CONDIMENTS

CONDIMENTS

*The Art of Buying, Making and Using
Mustards, Oils, Vinegars, Chutneys, Relishes,
Sauces, Savory Jellies and More*

KATHY GUNST

Illustrations by Keiko Narahashi

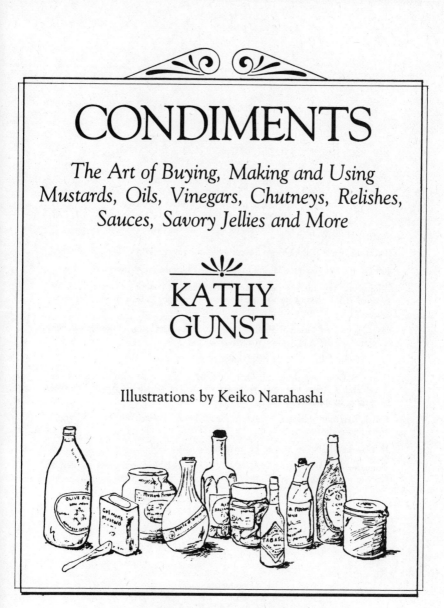

G. P. PUTNAM'S SONS/NEW YORK

To John

Sweet-and-Sour Red Cabbage Soup reprinted by permission of Sara Moulton.

Jim Fobel's Low-Sodium Mustard reprinted by permission of Jim Fobel.

"Nam Prik" reprinted by permission of The Putnam Publishing Group from *The Original Thai Cookbook* by Jennifer Brennan. Copyright © 1981 by Jennifer Brennan.

Jessica's Pickled Oriental Radishes reprinted by permission of Jessica Weber. Copyright © 1983 by Jessica Weber.

Apple Cider Jelly reprinted by permission of Kate Slate.

Breast of Duck in a Mustard, Orange, Champagne Sauce with Candied Lime Slices and Walnuts reprinted by permission of James Haller, Chef of The Blue Strawbery Restaurant in Portsmouth, New Hampshire.

Quick Ketchup reprinted by permission of Penny Potenz Winship. Copyright 1983 by Penny Potenz Winship.

Hot-Sweet Mustard reprinted by permission of Anne Montgomery.

Tomato-Apple Relish and Watermelon Rind Pickle reprinted by permission of Connie Weeks from *Using Summer's Bounty* by Connie Weeks.

Library of Congress Cataloging in Publication Data

Gunst, Kathy.
Condiments: the art of buying, making and using
mustards, oils, vinegars, chutneys, relishes, sauces,
savory jellies and more.

Includes index.
1. Condiments.   I. Title.
TX819.A1G86   1984   641.3'384   84-4759
ISBN 0-399-12919-7

ACKNOWLEDGMENTS

Thanks to everyone who lent their tastebuds and helped me decipher the good condiments from the bad: Gene Brown, Bill Bell, Sarah Grossman, Barry Cantor, Stanley Dorn, Jeff Rathaus, Jim Haller, Tom O'Brien, Stephanie Curtis, Kate Slate, Mardee Regan, Nancy Rudolph, Lucy Rudolph, Judy Wenning, Connie Weeks, Michael Gunst and Matt Lewis and Shelley Boris from Dean & Deluca.

Thanks to Robert Cornfield, my agent, for all his support, guidance and good ideas and to my editor, Diane Reverand, for believing in this project and giving me lots of good editorial advice.

Many thanks to the producers, manufacturers and cooks who introduced me to their wonderful products.

Thank you to Dorothee Kocks who spent long hours typing this manuscript and giving me positive feedback at a time when I really needed it.

Thank you to the editors at *Diversion* magazine who published my first article (on mustard) some seven years ago, and to the people at *Food & Wine* magazine for all their support and encouragement.

Also, thanks to Nancy and Lee Gunst and Leona and Leonard Levy who thought the idea of leaving college for a year and going off to cooking school wasn't so crazy after all.

And finally, thanks to Karen Frillmann for being a friend through it all and to John Rudolph, who loves condiments more than anyone else I know.

CONTENTS

INTRODUCTION

CONDIMENTS ARE TO FOOD what jewelry and makeup are to clothing. They are not essential; they won't keep you warm or well fed, but they definitely "dress up" your food and make eating a lot more interesting.

What exactly is a condiment? Mustard, chutney, relish and hot pepper sauce are condiments. But so are many oils and vinegars. Of course you can cook with an extra virgin olive oil or an aged wine vinegar, but these foods are at their best when they are used to embellish other dishes. And it is this ability, to complement the flavors in other foods, that distinguishes a condiment from an herb, spice or other raw ingredient.

Up until a few years ago, the only condiments you found in most people's refrigerators were mayonnaise, ketchup and bright yellow mustard. But recently the list has grown: Dijon mustard, Italian olive oil and Japanese soy sauce have also become staples. What most people don't realize is that there are hundreds of other wonderful condiments that can be bought or made. The whole point of this book is to help you discover them.

Have you ever tried a homemade peach chutney, laced with

ginger, spices and peppers, served with a spicy lamb curry? Or a Moroccan chile pepper sauce grilled on oysters; an oil made from the essence of hazelnuts sprinkled over a mixed green salad; or soy sauce, garlic, scallions and lime juice served as a dipping sauce with deep-fried shrimp?

Of course, condiments can also be served with simpler foods. A grainy mustard on a hot dog, homemade ketchup on a hamburger or pickled watermelon rind served with a sandwich. Condiments were originally created thousands of years ago to improve the flavor of everyday foods. The beauty of condiments is that they can make eating the same foods every day seem like a completely new experience each time.

In the last few years condiments have become "hot" items in specialty food shops and grocery stores. You can now choose from literally hundreds of mustards, oils, vinegars, chutneys, relishes, sauces and jellies from around the world. But should you spend $10 for a crock of fancy, imported mustard? Is it any better than the mustard you've been using for the past ten years? Is $25 too much for a bottle of extra virgin olive oil? Will it be worth it? The answer is yes, but only if you know which one to buy and how to use it.

Over the last year I've tasted hundreds of different condiments. And in each chapter, you'll find specific recommendations for those brands I consider superior *and* worth the price. Whenever possible, I've chosen brands that are free of preservatives and excessive amounts of salt and sugar. I've also given hints for how to use these condiments, recipes for cooking with them and, in many cases, recipes for making your own.

Making homemade condiments is very easy. Toward the end of the summer, when fruits, vegetables and herbs are abundant and inexpensive, I spend an entire day making chutneys, ketchups, relishes and pickles. Then in December, when everyone is going crazy trying to decide what to buy for Christmas, I take these condiments out of the pantry, put a homemade label on them and cover the jars with decorative fabric and ribbon. An old-fashioned mason jar filled with coconut chutney, a tall wine bottle of champagne vinegar with garden herbs, or a glass jar packed with an onion and cassis relish are some of the nicest gifts you can give.

By now you've probably realized that this is not a traditional cookbook. It's not a book that asks you to learn new techniques or cooking styles or to spend a lot of money. It is a book that asks you to be creative and a little bit adventurous with the foods you eat. I hope that the suggestions, ideas and recipes you find on the following pages will inspire you to create your own dishes and will help you use condiments to make eating a more pleasurable experience.

—KATHY GUNST
South Berwick, Maine
January 1984

Silver Mustard Pot
London, 1782

1
MUSTARD

"MY PANTRY IS FILLED with more than 200 mustards and my work has just begun . . ."

I found this sentence in a notebook I titled "Mustard Tasting Notes: 1982." It was written in a state of confusion and anxiety. Every time I thought I was getting a handle on the mustard market, it seemed to grow out from under me. At least once a week someone would call to announce that he or she had just discovered a new mustard that I simply had to taste to believe.

If you've looked into a specialty food shop (or even your local grocery store) lately, you know exactly what I'm talking about. What was once a simple matter of choosing between four or five different mustards is now a complex, multinational decision. There are now so many mustards on the market that you could spend months tasting them all, trying to figure out which ones have the best flavor and which are actually worth the often outrageous price.

The fact is that in recent years mustard has grown more in popularity than any other condiment or spice. There has been a deluge of fancy imports. And American mustard makers—both corporate ones and smaller cottage industries—have also reacted to the craze. Even the R. T. French Company, makers of that bright yellow all-American favorite since 1904, introduced a new deli-style and Dijon-style mustard a few years ago because, according to their research, "an increasing number of homes are now stocking more than one kind of mustard."

The variety of mustards available today is matched only by the number of theories about the origin of this spicy brown paste. Mustard seeds can be traced back as far as 3000 B.C. The ancient Egyptians, Greeks, Indians and Romans are all said to have grown mustard seeds and cooked the tender leaves of the mustard plant. (The Egyptians originally chewed the seeds whole while eating meat in order to give their food more flavor.) Mustard was eventually brought to Europe, where its popularity flourished. By the thirteenth century, "Mustarder" was a common occupation.

How mustard found its name is another hotly debated question. In classical times, mustard was made by mixing the pounded seeds with *mustum* (unfermented wine). The suffix "ard" is supposedly derived from the Teutonic "-hart," meaning hard, strong or intense—all characteristics of a good mustard. Another explanation is that the word "mustard" (or the French *"moutarde"*) comes from the Latin *mustum ardens*, meaning "burning must," since mustard seeds were mixed with grape must in early France.

A more romantic story is told by the people of Dijon, France. Long associated with fine mustard, the Dijonnais claim the word was established in the late part of the fourteenth century by Philip the Bold, the Duke of Burgundy. Local legend has it that the Duke had difficulty digesting meat during the lengthy and elaborate banquets he was so famous for giving. He asked his chef to devise a sauce that would disguise the meat's often rancid smell and taste. *Moult ma tarde*, meaning "a long time I delay my meal," was the term given to this spicy yellow condiment which allowed the Duke and his guests to savor their food. Later, this phrase was shortened to *moutarde*, the French word for mustard.

This story, apocryphal or not, gives some clue as to why mustard has remained so popular over the centuries. In the past, mustard was enjoyed simply because everyday foods weren't flavorful enough or had a downright bad taste. Early mustard users were not "gourmets." Today, despite its association with the "gourmet" and "specialty" food world, mustard is loved for similar reasons. Of all condiments, it is undoubtedly the most basic, capable of complementing and enhancing just about every type of savory food.

MUSTARD SURVEY

Our growing enthusiasm for mustard has produced an onslaught of new products and, not surprisingly, the results are varied. For each terrific new mustard I've tasted, there have been at least five "duds." I refer to these mustards as the "trendies"—mustards that are cute and brimming with interesting ingredients but, in the end, have absolutely no memorable qualities. Usually these trendies are packaged so beautifully that you'd be willing to bet money that they'll taste good; they just *look* so delicious. But looks can be deceptive. One spoonful and it's all over.

When tasting a mustard, the first thing I look for is pure mustard flavor—not salt, flour, oil or a strong herb taste, but mustard. After all, that's supposedly what you're buying. Far too many of the products I sampled were filled with ingredients that overwhelmed, or conflicted with, the natural flavor of the mustard seeds.

What follows is an attempt to make sense of the ever-growing selection of mustards. I've divided the mustards into nine major types, given specific recommendations for those products I feel are delicious (and worth the price), along with some hints on what they'll go best with.

American-Style Mustard

The word "style" in this category is significant. Although there is now a large (and impressive) selection of American mustards to choose from, what is truly defined as American-style mustard is *not* terribly impressive. But, like iceberg lettuce, American-style mustard has its place.

Everyone knows about this type of mustard. Its mild (some would say bland) taste and bright yellow color is a familiar childhood memory. In the midst of raving about all the new, exotic mustards on the market, we tend to forget about old favorites like Gulden's and Heinz.

American-style mustard breaks down into two basic categories: the smooth, bright yellow "ball park" mustard made from ground white seeds, vinegar, sugar and spices (most notably turmeric, a deep-yellow-colored spice used in curries); and the coarser, somewhat spicier brown "deli-style" mustard, made from a mixture of ground white and black seeds, vinegar and spices.

TASTING NOTES:
American mustards seem to have been made to be eaten with hot dogs. They are also a good accompaniment to delicatessen sandwiches, sausages and baked beans.

BEST BRANDS:

"Ball Park" Mustards
Gulden's Spicy Brown—Made from a mixture of black and white seeds, Gulden's is still terrific after all these years. It's the quintessential accompaniment to hot dogs; not bad with hamburgers, either.

French's Golden Yellow Mustard—I'm afraid I can't rave about this mustard. To me, it has absolutely no mustard flavor. But this is America's number-one-selling mustard, so someone must like it.

Deli-Style Mustards

Some of the very best deli mustards are those sold in local delicatessens and by hot dog and pretzel vendors. Every city has its favorites and, while these products aren't for sale nationwide, they are well worth seeking out.

French's Bold 'n Spicy—While hardly bold or spicy, this recent addition to the line of condiments from the R. T. French Company does have a more authentic mustard flavor than regular French's Yellow.

Kosciusko's Polish Mustard—Stone-ground from a blend of white and black seeds, this grainy mustard adds great flavor to sandwiches and sausages.

Dijon and Dijon-Style Mustard

As far as I'm concerned, nothing rivals a good Dijon mustard. It should be pungent and spicy with a smooth, creamy texture. The Dijonnais have an expression to describe the characteristics of a truly good mustard: *mont au nei*, meaning "coming up to the nose." It is also said in Dijon that mustard should "stimulate the appetite and aid digestion, but never burn the throat or alter the taste of sauces or dishes."

The Dijonnais take mustard making as seriously as some of their fellow Burgundians take wine making. And there are strict laws in France, some dating back as far as the late 1880s, that govern what can, and can not, go into a Dijon mustard.

According to French law, a Dijon mustard must be made exclusively from black seeds (*Brassica nigra*), salts and spices mixed with either white wine, *verjuice* (the juice of unripened grapes), or vinegar. By law, no sugars, flours, oils, perfumes, colorings or additives may be added. Any mustard that deviates from this traditional recipe must be called Dijon-style. Dijon mustard is made by crushing the hulled seeds into a yellow paste and then mixing them with the liquids and flavorings. The mustard is allowed to sit for three days to allow the heat and flavors to come together and then it is bottled. An average of 57,000 metric tons of Dijon mustard is made every year.

TASTING NOTES:
Of all varieties of mustard, Dijon is probably the most versatile. It's perfect served with steaks, leg of lamb, chicken, boiled beef, cold meats, sausages and fish. Try it as a base for vinaigrettes and use it for cooking; its smooth texture and pungent flavor blend easily into soups, stews and sauces.

BEST BRANDS:
Amora Dijon—Made in downtown Dijon, the Amora Company makes a delicious, traditional mustard.

Bocquet Yvetot—This wonderfully sharp Dijon comes in a decorative faience pot; a bit expensive but it makes a lovely gift.

Edmond Fallot's Moutarde de Dijon—The Fallot Company has been making this extremely hot and delicious mustard in Beaune, France, since 1840. Try a dollop on baked beans.

Étoile de Dijon (Richter Brothers)—An excellent, piquant Dijon. A bit overpriced because of the mason jar it's packed in, but worth it all the same.

French's Vive La Dijon!—Who would believe that an absolutely first-rate Dijon-style mustard could be produced in Rochester, New York? This mustard has the sharp flavor and creamy consistency that a real Dijon should. For under a dollar, it's very impressive stuff.

Grey Poupon—This is the only mustard made in the United States that is granted the status of "Dijon mustard." Although it's not nearly as good as its French counterparts, it is a moderately priced, well-flavored Dijon.

La Charcutière Dijon Mustard—This is a very reasonably priced mustard considering its wonderful, sharp flavor.

Old Monk Dijon Mustard—Although it doesn't have the usual hot "tweak" of Dijon, this is a delicious, mild mustard.

English Mustard (Powder)

For centuries, mustard has been a staple of the English kitchen. Thirteenth-century Tudor households were said to consume mustard in enormous quantities. The Earl of Northumberland, who apparently was not unlike the rest of his countrymen, would go through between 160 and 190 gallons of mustard a year.

English mustard powder as we know it today is credited to a woman named Mrs. Clements. The story goes that in 1720, she developed a powder that produced a smooth-textured mustard rather than the grainy type that was so typical throughout England. What was so revolutionary about her mustard was that she ground the seeds in a mill rather than crushing them with a mortar and pestle, and then she put the mustard flour through a sieve to remove the hulls. Mrs. Clements took her "discovery" from town to town and eventually to London, where it found favor with King George I. Soon mustard powder was made on a commercial basis throughout the country. It was referred to as "Durham mustard"—a tribute to Mrs. Clements' hometown.

The popularity of English mustard was furthered in 1814 when a miller named Jeremiah Colman bought a flour and mustard mill in Norwich, England. His company became so successful that, forty years later, he bought a larger factory in Carrow exclusively for producing his pungent mustard powder. Today, the world-famous Colman's mustard is still made in that same factory.

The English people have always preferred mustard in powder form. Made of a blend of ground black and white mustard seeds, wheat flour and spices, English mustard is terrifically hot. To make English mustard, simply add cold water to the powder, just enough to make a somewhat thick paste. It should sit for between ten and thirty minutes to develop full flavor and heat. (The full flavor develops after ten minutes and diminishes after a few hours.) You can also experiment by adding milk, cider, flat beer or herbs. Whatever liquid you choose, make sure it is cold; heat will kill the enzymes that activate the pungency and flavor.

TASTING NOTES:

English mustard is extremely versatile. There is no better accompaniment to roast beef or leftover roasts. It also makes a tangy glaze for baked ham and goes well with sausages and sharp cheeses. Since mustard powder acts as an emulsifier and preservative, it is often added to homemade mayonnaise; it not only adds a delicious flavor but prevents curdling and spoilage as well.

BEST BRANDS:

English Mustard Powder

Many specialty food shops and health food stores blend their own variety of mustard seeds and flours into a powder. These can be used in the same manner as any commercially made mustard powder.

Since 1814, the leading type of mustard powder has been Colman's. There are three types of Colman's powders to choose from:

Colman's Genuine Double Superfine is the hottest in the line; *Colman's Double Superfine* is a medium-to-hot powder; and *Colman's Special Mild Blend* is for those who want mustard flavor without the intense heat.

Prepared English Mustard

There are quite a few prepared English mustards on the market. I've found that very few of them are able to match the pure, hot flavor of the English mustard powders.

Colman's Prepared Mustard—This smooth mustard is not nearly as good as the Colman powders but has a good spicy bite nonetheless.

Isle of Arran Hot English Mustard—Made on the Isle of Arran off the coast of Scotland, this is a thick, hot-sweet mustard. Try it with ham and thinly sliced roast beef.

La Favorite Tewkesbury Mustard—Made in England, this smooth mustard is spiked with liberal amounts of fresh horseradish.

Flavored Mustard

Flavored mustards are essentially Dijon or Dijon-style mustards with the simple addition of an herb, spice or flavoring. You can buy just about every type of flavored mustard that you can possibly think of—and some you wouldn't want to. They range from a traditional tarragon-flavored mustard to more esoteric combinations, such as olives and anchovies or tomatoes, currants and beets.

My feeling about these mustards is that, for the most part, they are overpriced and unnecessary. Why is it that manufacturers feel they can charge a dollar or two more for a mustard by simply putting a sprig of fresh tarragon in it? Although some of these mustards do make nice gifts, they are just as easy to make on your own. If, for example, you want a lemon- or lime-flavored mustard, take some Dijon mustard and add a few teaspoons of fresh lemon or lime juice to taste and some grated zest (rind) for extra flavor. (See recipe for flavored mustard on page 35.)

TASTING NOTES:
- Add a tablespoon of flavored mustard to a basic oil and vinegar dressing.
- Try adding a touch of flavored mustard to homemade coleslaw or potato salad.
- Spread flavored mustard on sandwiches. Some of my favorite combinations include green peppercorn mustard and roast beef; herb-flavored mustard with chicken or turkey slices; champagne mustard with shrimp salad; tarragon-flavored mustard with chicken salad; and spicy mustard with a grilled-cheese sandwich.
- Serve with roast beef, ham, sausages and hamburgers.
- Flavored mustards add great flavor to grilled steaks, fish and bar-becued chicken.
- Mix flavored mustard with sour cream or yogurt to make a great dip for raw vegetables and grilled shrimp.
- Mix a spicy mustard with orange or lemon marmalade and use to glaze spareribs, chicken or duck.

BEST BRANDS:

All too often, these flavored mustards are heavy-handed; the added flavorings tend to overwhelm, or conflict with, the natural flavor of the mustard. There are, however, a few worth recommending:

Florida Champagne Mustard—Produced in the Champagne region of France, this mustard has a rich, full flavor that goes well with chicken, fish and beef. Made with white wine, it comes in tubes and Champagne-shaped bottles.

Isle of Arran's Crunchy Beer Mustard—Made on the Isle of Arran, off the coast of Scotland, this grainy mustard (the seeds have been left whole to give it a wonderful texture) has the rich, yeasty flavor of beer. Excellent on hamburgers and with steaks and sausages.

Marcel Recorbet's Mustard with Green Peppercorns—The sharp, biting flavor of crushed green peppercorns makes this smooth mustard an ideal accompaniment to cold poached salmon or shrimp; it also works well on duck and roast beef.

Old San Antonio Jalapeño Mustard—Leave it to the Texans to add hot, crunchy bits of jalapeño pepper to this delicious bright yellow American-style mustard. Try it on hot dogs and chile dogs.

Paul Corcellet's Peanut Mustard—This has a unique, rich, nutty taste. Surprisingly, the peanut flavor blends beautifully with the mustard. Try it as a dip with raw vegetables or in a Chinese-style chicken salad.

Paul Corcellet's Star Anise Mustard—If you like the flavor of anise (licorice), you'll probably love this; if you don't, stay far away. Makes a different tasting vinaigrette and adds a great flavor to a ham sandwich.

Pikarome's Green Peppercorn Mustard—The spicy, pungent flavor of crushed green peppercorns overwhelms this Dijon mustard in a most pleasing way. It's fantastic on hamburgers, cold chicken and a grilled steak.

German-Style Mustard

The Germans, like the French and the British, adore mustard—or, as they call it, *Senf*. Made from a blend of ground mustard seeds, wine vinegar, salt, sugar and spices, there are two major varieties of German mustard: *Bavarian*—a sweet, dark mustard; and the more popular *Düsseldorf*—a spicy mustard similar to Dijon.

TASTING NOTES:
German mustard, it seems, was made to be eaten with sausages and wurst. The Düsseldorf mustards, which range from mild to very sharp, hold up to all sorts of spicy sausages and salamis. And there is nothing better served with a steaming platter of sauerkraut, smoked pork and sausages. The sweet flavor of Bavarian mustard complements the more delicate sausages like *Weisswurst*, which is made from veal. German mustards, on the whole, are extremely reasonably priced.

BEST BRANDS:
Elsie's German Mustard—Elsie's is a small German restaurant located, of all places, in Falmouth, Massachusetts, on Cape Cod. Their homemade mustard is smooth and slightly pungent and goes well with sausages, dark bread and hot potato salad.
Frenzel's Senfli Düsseldorf Mustard—This mustard has a traditional, hearty flavor.
Hengstenberg's Rôtisseur—Hot and spicy, this mustard has a wonderful, crunchy texture; try it as a dip with raw vegetables or on a smoked ham sandwich.
Hengstenberg's Sweet Mustard—This Bavarian-style mustard is a bit sweet for some palates but adds good flavor to soups and cold meats.

Grainy Mustard

Grainy mustards, or what the French call *moutarde à l'ancienne*, taste like all mustards used to taste before the eighteenth-century innovation of removing the seed's hull. Made from a mixture of ground and semi-ground seeds combined with vinegar and spices, this mustard's greatest asset is its texture. Grainy mustards have a taste similar to Dijon, although they are generally not as sharp. Their texture ranges from somewhat creamy to thick and crunchy.

TASTING NOTES:
- Serve grainy mustards with cold meat platters.
- Use grainy mustards to add flavor and texture to sandwiches.
- Add a tablespoon of grainy mustard to a vinaigrette.
- Spread grainy mustard on a grilled steak, breast of duck or chicken and place under the broiler for a mustardy glaze.
- Serve with sautéed liver and onions.
- Serve a selection of grainy mustards with a platter of sweet and hot sausages.
- Add a tablespoon of grainy mustard to a potato and scallion salad or a homemade shrimp salad with orange slices.
- Broil a tablespoon or two of grainy mustard on a thick slice of French or Italian bread. Serve over a bowl of homemade onion, vegetable or pea soup.
- Serve one or two varieties of grainy mustard with a steaming hot platter of homemade corned beef and cabbage.

BEST BRANDS:
Boetje's Dutch Mustard—Made in Rock Island, Illinois, this mustard is very spicy with a subtle sweetness. It's terrific on sausages, salami and in vinaigrettes.

Edmond Fallot's Moutarde Old-Fashioned Grainy—This mustard, made of semi-ground and ground seeds, has a very, very spicy flavor. It's delicious spread on cold chicken, deviled eggs and mild cheeses.

Isle of Arran Original Mustard—Made on an island off the coast of Scotland, this slightly sweet mustard can only be described as crunchy. The whole grains of mustard are mixed with vinegar, honey and a touch of horseradish.

Moutarde de Meaux Pommery—According to the label, it was in 1760 that a superior of the ancient religious order of Meaux gave the Pommery family the "secret recipe" for this mustard. Brillat-Savarin, the renowned, late eighteenth-century French gastronomist, called it "the mustard for gourmets." Though it has a pleasant texture and mild taste, the more popular this mustard has become over the years, the more the flavor seems to decline. What would Brillat-Savarin say now?

Paul Corcellet's Grainy Mustard—This mustard has a wonderful crunchy texture with a tart flavor.

Plochman's Stone Ground Mustard—This is the most reasonably priced grainy mustard I've found. Made in Chicago by the Plochman family since 1852, it is a terrific combination of half-crushed seeds, vinegar and lots of fresh horseradish. Try mixing it with orange marmalade and basting a ham, duck or other bird.

Zatarain's Creole Mustard—Creole mustard is made from brown seeds that are steeped in distilled white vinegar, coarsely ground, and then left to marinate for twelve hours before being bottled. This piquant variety is a favorite throughout New Orleans and the South.

Hot Mustard

To some people, the key characteristic of a good mustard is just how hot it is. Manufacturers, catching on to this "macho" attitude, have begun producing mustards labeled specifically as "Hot," "Super Hot," et cetera. Generally, these are Dijon-style mustards with the addition of cayenne pepper, horseradish or chile peppers.

TASTING NOTES:
These mustards range from mildly spicy to "Oh-my-God-I-can't-stand-it" hot. Cooking with these mustards isn't always the best idea because they tend to overwhelm other flavors.

Those products marketed specifically as "Super Hot" are generally all heat and no flavor. My idea of a good hot mustard is a spicy Dijon or a freshly made English or Chinese mustard powder. However, the mustards listed below are also good and guaranteed to set your tongue on fire.

BEST BRANDS:
Chalif Hot 'n' Sweet Mustard—According to the label: "Shortly after the turn of the century, Louis Chalif, the first of the great ballet masters to leave Russia . . . emigrated to America. Two of Louis Chalif's most valued possessions were his ballet shoes and his recipe for mustard." Whether or not this story is true is not important; this is excellent mustard. It is very hot and spicy with a subtle degree of sweetness. Use as a glaze on ham or roast lamb or as a dip for beef fondue and raw vegetables. It's also terrific mixed with mayonnaise to make a pungent egg or chicken salad.

Inniemore Scotch Mustard—Made in Wales, this spicy concoction is fired up with chile vinegar, chile peppers and cayenne pepper; it has a pleasing grainy consistency.

Military Mustard—This thick mustard, made in the West Highlands of Scotland, reminds me of a hot mustard chutney. It's excellent on roast beef or a cheese sandwich.

Oriental Mustard

Anyone who has ever been to a Chinese restaurant is familiar with *Gai Lot,* the bright yellow, fiery hot mustard that's served with every meal. Made from the very spicy brown seed called *Brassica juncea,* it's mustard that can make you feel, if only for a moment, that you'll never, ever, have sinus problems again.

[28]

Prepared Chinese mustard is available in jars, but it never seems to have the same impact as the powdered variety. For the real thing, Chinese mustard must be made fresh from equal quantities of ground powder and cold water. Like English mustard powder, it should sit for anywhere between ten and thirty minutes to develop full heat and flavor before serving.

Despite popular misconceptions, the hot, pale green stuff that accompanies *sushi*, *sashimi* and many other Japanese dishes is not mustard; it is called *wasabi* and is made from ground green horse-radish root (see page 127). There is, however, a Japanese mustard called *karashi*. It's a very strong ground mustard powder that is mixed with water like English mustard powders. *Karashi* is sold in powder form and ready-made in tubes. It is generally used in soy-based dipping sauces and served with dumplings, salads and sea-food. Use it sparingly; it's very potent stuff.

TASTING NOTES:
Oriental mustard is traditionally used as a dip with egg rolls or spring rolls. It's also delicious served with dumplings, spareribs, Chinese-style steamed fish and noodle dishes.

BEST BRANDS:
If you live near a Chinese area, check with a Chinese grocery store for their own blend of mustard powder. If you can't find any, English mustard powder can easily be substituted. Here are a few recommended Chinese powders:

Dynasty; S & B; China Bowl Mustard Powder.

Prepared Oriental Mustards
China Bowl Chinese Hot Mustard Sauce—Made in Hong Kong from milled Oriental mustard seeds, spices and Chinese white rice vinegar, this mustard has a definite bite. It's thick, spicy and won-derful with barbecued spareribs, dumplings and in Chinese-style sauces.

[29]

House Mustard (Neri Karashi)—Sold in small tubes, this spicy mustard is made in Osaka, Japan. Add a teaspoon to some soy sauce along with some grated ginger to make a great dipping sauce for seafood and dumplings.

Roland Chinese Hot Mustard—This is hot, but not too hot. Use with roast pork and *dim sum*. Mix a little into a chicken salad with scallions, peanuts and grated ginger.

Sweet Mustard

I have a problem with this type of mustard, since I don't particularly like my mustard sweet. However, it's quite obvious that more than a few people disagree because the number of sweet mustards on the market seems to double every year. The favorite sweetening ingredient is honey, but white sugar, brown sugar and corn syrup are also used. The result is successful only if the basic mustard possesses enough character of its own. Unfortunately, many of these mustards are simply overwhelmed by sweeteners.

The Swedes are extremely fond of sweet mustards. Aside from a few slightly spicy, grainy mustards, the majority of the Swedish mustards that make their way to American markets are very sweet.

TASTING NOTES:
These mustards range from slightly sweet to gooey, cotton-candy sweet. Generally, they are not very hot, although there are some mustards that are labeled "Sweet-Hot."

Sweet mustards pair particularly well with smoked fish, smoked turkey and smoked meat, like Smithfield ham. The popular Swedish dish *Gravlax* is traditionally served with a sweet mustard-dill sauce. Some people like to mix sweet mustards with sour cream and use as a dip.

BEST BRANDS:

Crabtree & Evelyn's Honey Mustard—This grainy mustard has just a subtle touch of sweetness that complements food without overwhelming it.

Honeycup Mustard—A wonderful balance of mustard and honey, this thick, sharp mustard is ideal for cooking; use it as a glaze on duck or take a tablespoon and grill it on strips of thick-slab bacon.

Sable & Rosenfeld Russian Style Prepared Mustard—This thick, butterscotch-colored mustard is ultra-sweet. It's superb as a glaze for ham or ribs, or as a spread for sandwiches.

Slotts Spicy Swedish Mustard—This Swedish favorite is only slightly hot with a very sugary flavor. It goes particularly well with smoked fish, ham and boiled shrimp.

The Silver Palate's Rough and Sweet Mustard—This mustard is wonderful. It has a sweet and spicy mustard-honey flavor with a thick, gooey consistency. Use as a glaze on a baked ham or on sandwiches. It's good enough to eat by itself.

MAKING YOUR OWN MUSTARD

Making mustard is a surprisingly straightforward process of grinding and mixing mustard seeds with a few other ingredients. Just what combination of seeds you use, what liquid you choose (water, vinegar, wine, beer, milk, and so forth) and what herbs, spices and flavorings you add determines what sort of mustard you'll end up with.

When making mustard you should realize that the seeds themselves are not hot until they are ground and moistened with some sort of cold liquid. The liquid activates a mixture of enzymes called myrosin, which is what gives the mustard its pungency.

Freshly made mustard is searingly hot. It should be allowed to sit for between ten to thirty minutes to develop flavor and allow the heat to subside slightly. The longer the mustard sits, the mellower it becomes.

The business of making mustard—both on a commercial basis and at home—invariably involves secrets. Take a look at the labels on a dozen jars of Dijon mustard and you'll see what I mean. Though they all list the same ingredients (mustard seeds, vinegar, salt and spices), they taste very different. It is the manufacturer's special combination of seeds and seasonings that gives each mustard its distinctive flavor.

All mustard comes from the same family, the *Cruciferae* plant—so called because it bears flowers with four petals arranged in the shape of a cross. From this plant come three different types of seeds, the basis of all mustard.

The most common is the white seed (*Brassica alba*), which is actually a yellowish-tan color. This is the mildest seed and is used to make American-style mustards and as a filler with spicier blends. It is also frequently used for making pickles and relishes because of its strong preservative powers.

Brassica nigra or black seed (actually a dark reddish-brown color) has been known since the earliest times for its potency. Black seeds are far spicier than the white seeds and are used for making hot mustards, most notably those produced in Dijon, France.

The third variety, *Brassica juncea* or brown seed, is the hottest of them all. Found throughout the Orient, this seed is said to be so hot that it actually repels insects while growing. This variety of seed is not generally used in prepared mustards but is frequently used in curries and ground into powder form to make what we call Chinese mustard. It's also used to make mustard oil, a spicy cooking oil sold in shops specializing in Indian foods.

The following homemade mustards should be stored in a glass jar in the refrigerator; they will keep about two to four weeks.

Anne Montgomery's Hot-Sweet Mustard

This mustard is simple to make but needs to sit overnight, so plan accordingly. It has a slightly sweet, spicy flavor. If you don't like your mustard sweet, simply cut the amount of sugar in half. Use on sandwiches, with grilled chicken and sausages.

¼ cup dry mustard powder
¼ cup white wine vinegar
⅓ cup dry white wine
1 tablespoon sugar
1 teaspoon salt
2 egg yolks, beaten

In a medium-size bowl, whisk together the mustard powder, vinegar, wine, sugar and salt. Cover and let sit overnight. Place the bowl over a pot of simmering water or transfer the mustard to the top of a double boiler. Whisk in the egg yolks and continue whisking until the mustard becomes thick and creamy, about 3 to 5 minutes. Let cool for at least an hour before serving. *Makes about 1 cup.*

Jim Fobel's Low-Sodium Mustard

If you read their labels, you will notice that most prepared mustards are loaded with salt. This recipe, created by Jim Fobel, author of *Beautiful Food* (Van Nostrand Reinhold), combines mustard seeds with powdered mustard, herbs and other flavorings—without a trace of salt. It's delicious on baked chicken, sandwiches, or as a base for a mustard vinaigrette. This mustard is best prepared a day ahead of time.

  3 tablespoons yellow mustard seeds
  2 tablespoons mustard powder
  1½ teaspoons turmeric
  1 teaspoon tarragon
  ¼ teaspoon cinnamon
  ⅔ cup water
  ¼ cup plus 2 teaspoons white distilled vinegar
  ¼ cup dry white wine
  2 tablespoons sugar
  2 tablespoons olive or vegetable oil
  1 garlic clove, minced

In a small, heavy stainless-steel saucepan, combine the mustard seeds, the mustard powder, the turmeric, tarragon and cinnamon. Add the water and stir to dissolve the mustard. Bring to a boil over a high heat, stirring constantly. Remove from the heat, cover and let stand for 8 hours or overnight.

Add ¼ cup of the vinegar, the wine, sugar, oil and garlic and bring to a boil over a high heat. Reduce the heat to low and simmer, stirring frequently, for 5 minutes.

Puree the mustard in a food processor or blender. Transfer to a small bowl and let cool to room temperature. Stir in the remaining 2 teaspoons of vinegar and taste for seasoning. If you like your mustard hot, stir in up to one additional teaspoon of powdered mustard. Cover and refrigerate for up to two weeks. *Makes about ⅔ cup.*

Herb-Flavored Mustard

I was inspired to create my own herb-flavored mustard after sampling more than a dozen different bottled varieties which all tasted much too artificial and overbearing. This simple recipe uses a prepared Dijon mustard as its base. It can easily be made with any combination of dried or fresh herbs and herb-flavored vinegar.

½ cup Dijon mustard
   About 2 teaspoons chopped fresh tarragon, rosemary, basil, thyme, oregano or sage, or 1 teaspoon dried
   About 1 teaspoon tarragon-flavored vinegar, or any other herb-flavored vinegar

Place the mustard into a medium-size serving bowl and stir in the herbs and vinegar. Mix well and taste for seasoning. Let sit for 10 minutes before serving. *Makes ½ cup.*

COOKING WITH MUSTARD

Mustard-Maple Glaze

This recipe provides enough glaze for 4 pork chops or 1 pound of scallops or shrimp. You can also double (or triple) the recipe and use on duck or ham.

Simply add the glaze during the last few minutes of cooking and place the dish under the broiler for 2 to 4 minutes before serving.

        3   tablespoons grainy, hot, or Dijon mustard
        2½   tablespoons maple syrup
        2   tablespoons orange juice
        2   teaspoons apple cider

Combine all ingredients. In a small stainless-steel saucepan, bring the glaze to a boil over a high heat. Reduce the heat and let simmer for 5 to 7 minutes, or until thickened and reduced to about ½ cup.

Mustard-Cider Cream Sauce

This is a rich, pungent sauce, based on an old Shaker recipe from the Hancock Shaker Village in Massachusetts. It's incredibly good served with smoked fish (particularly trout), ham or roast beef. Make it at least 15 minutes before serving.

¾ cup heavy cream
¼ cup brown sugar
2 tablespoons mustard powder
⅓ cup fresh apple cider
½ tablespoon cider vinegar
⅛ teaspoon salt
1 egg yolk

Heat ½ cup of the cream with the sugar in the top half of a double boiler set over barely simmering water (or in a medium saucepan set over simmering water) until warm.

In a small bowl, mix the mustard powder, cider, vinegar and salt. Using a whisk, gradually beat the mustard-cider mixture into the warmed cream.

Beat the egg yolk slightly in a small bowl. Add 3 tablespoons of the mustard-cream to the yolk, mix well and gradually add it back to the saucepan. Cook the sauce over a low heat, whisking frequently, for about 5 minutes or until the sauce begins to thicken. Remove from the heat and let cool.

Whip the remaining ¼ cup of cream until soft peaks form. Gently fold the whipped cream into the mustard and let sit for about 15 minutes before serving. *Makes 1½ cups.*

Scandinavian Mustard-Dill Sauce

Serve this sauce with an assortment of herring, *Gravlax* or smoked fish. It also adds a sweet, pungent flavor to a new potato and chopped scallion salad.

⅓ cup Dijon mustard
2 tablespoons sugar
3 tablespoons white wine vinegar
¾ cup vegetable oil
⅓ cup minced fresh dill
Salt and pepper to taste

In a small bowl, whisk together the mustard, sugar and vinegar until well blended. Gradually beat in the oil until blended and smooth. Stir in the dill and add salt and pepper to taste. Cover and refrigerate an hour before serving. *Makes about 1 cup.*

Mustard Vinaigrette

You can use any type of mustard you want with this vinaigrette; the classic ingredient, however, is Dijon mustard. This dressing is wonderful served over a mixed green salad, over steamed asparagus with a sprinkling of capers and finely chopped hard-boiled egg, or with a simple chicken salad.

1 teaspoon Dijon, grainy or herb-flavored mustard
3 tablespoons olive oil
2 tablespoons red or white wine vinegar
Salt and pepper to taste

Whisk together all the ingredients and serve. *Makes about ½ cup.*

Broiled Salmon with Mustard-Hazelnut Butter

2½ teaspoons hazelnut oil (see page 86)
2 salmon steaks, about 1½ inches thick
2 tablespoons butter, softened
1 tablespoon grainy or Dijon mustard
1 tablespoon fresh lemon juice
1 tablespoon finely chopped hazelnuts or almonds
  (optional)
Lemon wedges

Grease a small baking pan or Pyrex dish with 1½ teaspoons of the oil. Place the salmon in the pan and preheat the broiler.

In a small bowl, mix the butter, mustard, lemon juice, hazelnuts and remaining 1 teaspoon of oil. Spread the flavored butter equally on the salmon steaks. Place the salmon about 4 inches from the heat and broil for 12 to 15 minutes, or until tender when tested with a fork.

Remove the salmon to a serving plate and spoon the pan juices on top. Serve with roasted potatoes or boiled new potatoes. *Serves 2.*

London, 1800

[39]

Pork Chops in a Mustard-Cider Sauce

This is a simple, hearty dish that is delicious served with red cabbage and roasted or pan-fried potatoes. It can be made more elegant by substituting slices of pork tenderloin (about 1½ inches thick) for the pork chops.

> 1 teaspoon olive or vegetable oil
> 2 cloves garlic, finely minced
> 2 lean pork chops, center cut
> 4 tablespoons Dijon mustard
> 1 teaspoon sage, crumbled
> Freshly ground black pepper
> 1 cup fresh apple cider

In a medium-size skillet, heat the oil over moderately high heat until it begins to get hot. Add the garlic and sauté just until it begins to turn a golden color. Add the pork chops and brown on both sides.

Raise the heat to high and spread each pork chop with ½ tablespoon of the mustard and ¼ teaspoon of the sage and some pepper. Turn the chops over and repeat. Add ½ cup of the cider to the skillet and let the mixture come to a boil. Reduce the heat to moderate; whisk in a tablespoon of the mustard, and let cook for 20 to 30 minutes, depending on the thickness of the chops, until just cooked and tender, turning frequently. Check to make sure the cider doesn't evaporate completely; add additional cider if necessary.

Raise the heat to high and add the remaining ½ cup of cider. Reduce to a syrupy glaze, turning the pork frequently. Whisk in the remaining tablespoon of mustard, heat and serve. *Serves 2.*

Mustard Butter

Add a tablespoon of this pungent mustard butter to grilled steaks and chops, pan-fried fish and sautéed shrimp and oysters.

    4 tablespoons unsalted butter, at room temperature
    1 teaspoon white mustard seeds, slightly crushed
    1 teaspoon mustard powder
    1 tablespoon dry white wine
    ¼ teaspoon salt
    ⅛ teaspoon freshly ground black pepper

In a small bowl, cream the butter until soft. Add the crushed mustard seeds, mustard powder, wine, salt and pepper and mix until smooth. Place some flour on your hands and shape the butter into a roll or log. Place in wax paper and refrigerate or freeze until ready to serve. *Makes about ¼ cup.*

Breast of Duck in a Mustard, Orange, Champagne Sauce with Candied Lime Slices and Walnuts

This wonderful dish was created by Jim Haller, a close friend and chef of The Blue Strawbery Restaurant in Portsmouth, New Hampshire. It's perfect for a small dinner party because you can make the sauce and the lime garnish ahead of time and wait until your guests arrive to bake the duck.

THE SAUCE

½ cup Dijon mustard
½ cup grainy mustard
1 cup orange marmalade
4 tablespoons frozen orange juice concentrate
1 cup melted butter
1 cup dry Champagne, or white wine
1 tablespoon freshly grated nutmeg
½ cup walnut halves

THE GARNISH

2 limes
1 cup water
1 cup sugar

THE DUCK

4 duck breasts, about ¾ to 1 pound each

Prepare the sauce: Place all the ingredients for the sauce, except the walnuts, into a blender or food processor and blend until smooth; you'll have about 3 cups. Place the sauce into a medium saucepan and simmer over a moderately high heat for about 30 minutes, or until reduced to 2 cups. Remove the sauce from the heat, stir in the walnuts and set aside.

Prepare the garnish: Thinly slice the limes and place in a medium-size saucepan with the water and the sugar. Simmer over moderate heat until the lime slices are coated in a thick syrup, about 10 minutes. Let sit until ready to serve.

Prepare the duck: Preheat the oven to 500° Fahrenheit. Place the duck breasts on a rack in a large baking pan. Bake for 20 minutes and remove from the oven. Reduce the heat to 350° and drain off all the fat that has accumulated in the bottom of the pan. Place the duck in the baking pan and cover with some of the sauce. Bake an additional 15 minutes. Remove from the oven and garnish each duck breast with 2 or 3 slices of lime. Serve with the additional sauce on the side. *Serves 4.*

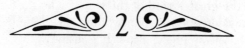

2

VINEGAR

In Japan and China, it's made from rice wine. In the United States, the main ingredient is apple cider, and in Mexico, cactus leaves or pineapple are used. Throughout Europe, wine and sherry are preferred, and in Sri Lanka, a Buddhist country where alcohol is forbidden, it is made from coconuts.

The word "vinegar" comes from the French words *"vin"* and *"aigre,"* meaning "soured wine." When wine, or any other naturally fermented alcohol (such as beer or hard cider) is exposed to air, it gradually turns to vinegar. The pungent, tart flavor of vinegar has been greatly welcomed by all who have come upon it.

The discovery of vinegar was, in all probability, an accident. Who it was that actually made this discovery is not known, but it surely happened many centuries ago. The Bible is filled with almost as many references to vinegar as it is to wine. The Chinese are known to have made rice wine vinegar over 3,000 years ago. And early drawings show that the Greeks and Romans created elaborate vessels to hold their vinegar into which chunks of crusty bread were dipped.

The business of making and bottling vinegar, however, didn't begin until the fourteenth century in France. In the Middle Ages, vinegar was the great hazard of the wine trade. At first, the soured wine was considered a loss, but it didn't take long before someone turned this "useless" liquid into a big business.

In the wine depot at Orléans, the demand for vinegar was so great that a guild of professional vinegar makers, the *Corporatif des Maîtres-Vinaigriers d'Orléans*, was established in 1394. Today, the best vinegars are still made using the old "Orléans process."

The process begins with the best ingredients—top-quality wine for wine vinegar and fresh, whole apples for apple cider vinegar. The liquid is placed into large wooden casks with small air holes. It is allowed to mature slowly and naturally until a film of bacteria (called the "mother") forms on top. The "mother" is the life force that keeps the vinegar alive and reproducing, generation after generation. At first it looks like a thick, white film. But as it matures, the "mother" grows into a gelatinous, slimy-looking thing that resembles a jellyfish.

Like good wine, the best vinegars are allowed to age properly, sometimes for several years. During the aging process, acetic acid is formed, which gives the vinegar its tartness. (Acetic acid is simply the natural chemical that forms when wine or any other naturally fermented alcoholic beverage is allowed to sour.) The vinegar is then drawn off with a spigot at the bottom of the cask, carefully so as not to kill the "mother." The cask is then replenished with a fresh batch of liquid.

That is the old-fashioned method. Today, there are many vinegar producers who use modern, high-tech equipment that enables this entire process to occur in about three days. The wine (or other ingredient) is usually of poor quality; it is sprinkled with wood chips to induce a "mother" and then heated at extremely high temperatures and aerated mechanically. While some of these "quick" vinegars are fine for recipes that call for only a teaspoon of vinegar, they can't compare with the flavor of those vinegars that are allowed to age slowly and naturally.

When buying vinegar there is an easy way to tell which process has been used. If the vinegar has been properly aged, the label will indicate "Made by the Orléans Process," "Aged in Wood," or "Vinaigre à l'Ancienne." Many of the vinegar producers tell you their whole production story right on the label.

The other thing to look for is the level of acidity in the vinegar. By law, this must be printed on the label. The strength of acidity varies greatly; the higher the level, the more tart the vinegar. Generally, the highest-quality vinegars have a high acidity level of six or seven percent compared to conventional supermarket brands with only four or five percent acidity.

VINEGAR SURVEY

Vinegar has come full circle. Centuries ago, it was considered a precious condiment fit for kings and queens. But with time, vinegar became an everyday household item and the quality suffered accordingly. Happily, vinegar's popularity and quality are on the upswing once again.

Today at grocery stores and specialty food shops you can buy vinegars from around the world. The variations are endless—ranging from a sweet red rice vinegar made in China to a Cabernet Sauvignon grape vinegar produced in the Napa Valley of California. And, not surprisingly, the range in price is equally diverse—from 39 cents for a bottle of white distilled supermarket vinegar to over $100 for a bottle of well-aged Italian balsamic vinegar.

What follows is a survey of the major types of vinegar, along with recommendations for those products that are superior and hints on how to use them and cook with them. In some cases, the price of the vinegar outweighs its quality, so I've given directions for making your own.

Apple Cider Vinegar

The early American colonists are said to have "invented" apple cider vinegar by allowing the natural sugars in apple cider to ferment—first into alcohol (or what they called "hard cider") and then into vinegar. Its most common use was for pickling vegetables, but apple cider vinegar was also used as a condiment—sprinkled into sweet soups, hearty stews, cold fruit "salads," hot fruit compotes and over steamed fresh vegetables.

Its pungent, apple flavor was not its only appeal. For years, apple cider vinegar was used to fight the common cold, arthritis and other ailments. Some New Englanders still use it as a tonic to help aid digestion.

Today apple cider vinegar is one of the biggest-selling vinegars in the country. Although many people consider its strong preservative powers and its inexpensive price tag to be its main attributes, a well-made apple cider vinegar can easily rival a wine vinegar. When properly aged, apple cider vinegar has a beautiful amber color and the fresh, tart flavor of apples.

There are great differences between a fine apple cider vinegar and the odorless, tasteless stuff you find on most supermarket shelves. To begin with, a good producer will start with a wide variety of whole apples; the more types of apples that go into the vinegar, the fuller the final flavor. (Most of the cheaper brands are made from apple cores and peelings.) The apples are first ground into a sauce and then cold-pressed to extract cider. The fresh cider is placed in wooden casks where the natural sugars ferment into alcohol, or hard cider. The hard cider is transferred to other wooden casks where it is exposed to air and gradually turns to vinegar. It is allowed to age in the casks until the vinegar has mellowed and developed a full, rich flavor.

Most of the cheaper, harsher-tasting brands are artificially infused with oxygen and then bottled without being aged. Read the label to make sure you have bought a quality vinegar; it should indicate "Made from Whole Apples Exclusively," and "Aged in Wood." You also want to look for a vinegar that is full-strength—five to five and a half percent acidity. Some of the best apple cider vinegars can be found in natural food stores. Also, many apple orchards across the country use leftover apples (and apple cider) to make vinegar. Check with your local orchard to see if they sell cider vinegar.

TASTING NOTES:
- Apple cider vinegar is delicious in salads—particularly potato salad and coleslaw.
- Add apple cider vinegar to a pumpkin soup or a rich vegetable stew. It wakes up the natural flavors of the vegetables and adds a great pungent flavor.
- Use cider vinegar as a base for homemade herb- and fruit-flavored vinegars; see page 65 for recipe.
- Add to homemade pickles and chutneys; see chapters 7 and 8 for recipes.
- Try making your own apple cider vinegar. It's surprisingly easy; the recipe is on page 69.

BEST BRANDS:
Beaufor Cider Vinegar—Made in France, this vinegar has been aged in oak casks for several years. It has a good, fresh apple flavor.

Paul Corcellet Cider Vinegar—This is an excellent French vinegar that has a pleasingly tart taste.

Soleillou Cider Vinegar with Peppercorns—Black, green and white peppercorns add a delicious "bite" to this well-flavored apple cider vinegar. Made in France, it's superb in salads and for cooking with.

Sterling Apple Cider Vinegar—Made exclusively from the juice of whole, fresh apples, this is one of the finest apple cider vinegars available. The Hildick family of Sterling, Massachusetts, has been making it since 1911.

Walnut Acres Apple Cider Vinegar—Made from organically grown apples, this is a wonderful, fresh-tasting vinegar.

[47]

Balsamic Vinegar

Aceto balsamico is to vinegar what the Ferrari or Maserati is to cars. *"Aceto,"* the Italian word for vinegar, and *"balsamico,"* which loosely translated means "that which is good for your health," is unlike any other type of vinegar. It has been made in and around the city of Modena, in the Emilia-Romagna region, for at least a millennium. According to Waverley Root, in his book *The Food of Italy*, "The earliest reference to [*aceto balsamico*] dates from 1046, when Bonifacio di Canossa presented a barrel of it to Emperor Henry III as a coronation gift."

Aceto balsamico is a rich, dark-brown vinegar that is so intensely aromatic and naturally sweet that it is sometimes used alone as a salad dressing or splashed over fresh strawberries. It has a sweet-and-sour flavor that is so refined you can drink it straight from the bottle.

Aceto balsamico is made exclusively from the must of wine grapes that contain a high sugar content, like Lambrusco, Salamino and white Trebbiano. The newly pressed must is filtered through cloth and then reduced by cooking it slowly in copper cauldrons. After the must is cooled, it is transferred to large barrels made of various select woods. (By Italian law, the casks can be made only of oak, chestnut, mulberry or juniper.) Once in the barrels, the must is exposed to air and the sugars ferment into alcohol and finally into vinegar. The vinegar is then transferred, about once a year, to barrels made of different types of wood. To be called *aceto balsamico*, Italian law says that the vinegar must age a minimum of three years, but most of the old Modenese family vinegars are aged for closer to 50 or 100 years.

Ever since it was first made, the Italians have considered balsamic vinegar a precious commodity. In *The Food of Italy*, Root writes: "In 1944, when the frantically clanging bells of the Ghirlandina warned Modena that American bombers were approaching, thousands took to bicycles and pedaled desperately out of the city. Many of them had time to scoop up money, jewels and other easy-

[48]

to-carry valuables; and on dozens of luggage carriers small kegs were strapped. They contained vinegar."

According to Burton Anderson, a noted expert on Italian wines and food, "The oldest balsamic vinegars—50, 100, 150, even 250 to 300 years old—are among the world's most expensive food products, rivaling caviar, truffles, certain ancient wines and Cognacs in value per gram . . . the oldest and finest *aceto balsamico* is for all practical purposes priceless, not for sale . . . Consider the words of Mino Durand as printed in the Italian newspaper *Corriere della Sera:* 'It costs as much as liquid gold but is even more precious and he who has it won't sell it but keeps it for himself, for his children, for his grandchildren, for a few dearest friends; one might give some to the surgeon who arises in the middle of the night to operate on one's wife . . . and who, emerging at twilight from the operating room, doesn't want money but asks only for a vial of the antique elixir.'"

TASTING NOTES:

There is a kind of ritual I go through when turning friends on to balsamic vinegar for the first time. First I ask them to smell it. The aroma is rich and full, without making your glands pucker up like other vinegars do. Then I pour a little of the vinegar into a spoon. As soon as they taste it, people go wild. (It's amazing how many of them want another spoonful.) Try it. You'll quickly understand why balsamic vinegar costs more than other vinegars. Listed below are just a few of my favorite ways to use balsamic vinegar:

• Balsamic vinegar is stronger than most other vinegars—you only need to use a little. Because it is so full-flavored and naturally sweet, you can use it alone on salads without oil; it's terrific for people who are counting calories.
• Fill an avocado half with some balsamic vinegar and a touch of extra virgin olive oil.
• Try broiling a slice of crusty Italian or French bread topped with balsamic vinegar, a little olive oil and chopped garlic.
• Add a teaspoon of balsamic vinegar to an oyster or clam on the

half shell and place it under the broiler for a few minutes until browned.

- Use balsamic vinegar to marinate meats and chicken.
- Use balsamic vinegar to deglaze pan juices from chicken, meat or fish dishes.
- Slice an assortment of fresh wild mushrooms and toss with balsamic vinegar, olive oil and a touch of walnut oil.
- Pour the vinegar over a bowl of strawberries or a fresh fruit salad.
- For centuries, Italians have been using balsamic vinegar as a refreshing drink. Pour a glass of seltzer or club soda and add a tablespoon of balsamic vinegar, a touch of sugar and a thin sliver of lemon peel.

BEST BRANDS:
Aceto Balsamico Fini—This has got to be the greatest vinegar in the world. Sometimes in the middle of the day, I'll sneak into the pantry for a taste. The Fini family has been making vinegar in their factory right outside Modena since the early 1600s. Their balsamic vinegar has become so popular in the United States that they can barely keep up with the demand. There are now two types of Fini vinegar: the silver labeled, which has been aged for seven years, and the gold labeled, which is aged for over fifteen years. They are remarkable vinegars.

Balsamico Reggiano Tradizionale—Aged for eighty years, this is very intense stuff. It costs about $40 for a 3.9-ounce bottle, but it should last you quite a while—a drop or two of this vinegar is equal to a cup of most other vinegars.

Balsamic Vinegar: Duke of Modena Reserve—Balsamic vinegar is also referred to as *aceto del duca,* recalling the colorful Duke of Este who made Modena his capital in 1596. This vinegar, produced by Grosoli Adriano in Modena, has a rich, delicious flavor. It is sold in regular bottles and in cruet-shaped gift bottles.

Balsamic Vinegar of Modena—Produced by Federzoni Elio e Co., this is the least expensive type of balsamic vinegar on the market. (A 17-ounce bottle costs about $3.) Although it doesn't approach Fini vinegar, it adds good flavor to salad dressings and marinades.

Bel Canto Balsamic Vinegar of Modena—This is a terrific vinegar. It comes in a tall, thin bottle and has the refined and sophisticated flavor that a balsamic vinegar should.

Chinese Vinegars

The Chinese are passionate about the sweet-and-sour flavor of rice vinegar, which they have been using for thousands of years. Although vinegar is used as a cooking ingredient in a wide variety of Chinese dishes, it is most frequently used as a condiment. The three major types of Chinese vinegar are red, black and white; in general, they are all sweeter and sharper than the delicate Japanese rice vinegars. They can be found in Oriental grocery stores and specialty food shops.

Chinese Red Vinegar

Made from red rice, this sweet vinegar is used for two reasons: to cut the richness of certain foods and to highlight the sweetness in soups, stews and seafood. One of the most extravagant uses for red vinegar is to add a tablespoon to a bowl of hot shark's fin soup—a super rich broth made with the thin strands of meat that are removed from a shark's fin. Another traditional specialty, steamed Chinese crabs, is almost always accompanied by a small dish of red vinegar; the sweetness of the vinegar enhances the crab meat beautifully. Red vinegar can also be used as a dip for oysters on the half shell, spring rolls, steamed dumplings and fried shrimp. It also makes a delicious vinaigrette mixed with pure Chinese peanut oil and chopped scallions.

[51]

BEST BRANDS:

Koon Chun Sauce Factory Red Vinegar—This vinegar, made from red rice, has a sweet, tart flavor. It's from Hong Kong and makes a wonderful dipping sauce for steamed crabs.

Tung Chun Red Vinegar—Try this Chinese vinegar mixed with peanut oil and grapefruit juice and serve with a watercress salad.

Chinese Black Vinegar

This dark-brown vinegar has a rich, sweet flavor that is similar to a Spanish sherry vinegar or an Italian balsamic vinegar. Black vinegar is believed to restore strength; in southern China it is made into a tonic and served to women after childbirth.

Like Chinese red vinegar, black vinegar is used to balance overly rich or sweet dishes. You can buy plain black vinegar or several varieties of extra-sweet, seasoned black vinegar.

BEST BRANDS:

Koon Chun Sauce Factory Black Vinegar—Made in China, this vinegar is tart and slightly sweet. It adds a pungent flavor to soups and stews.

Pat Chun Company's Chinese Black Vinegar—Made in Hong Kong, this sweetened black vinegar is flavored with sugar, cloves, orange peel and ginger. It smells like Christmas and has a wonderful, spicy taste. Sweet and syrupy, it makes a tasty sauce for grilled shrimp, a marinade for duck, and adds flavor to soups, stews and casseroles. Try sprinkling a little over fresh raspberries or a slice of ripe melon.

Tung Chun Black Vinegar—This tart vinegar is ideal for cooking, particularly with sweet-and-sour dishes.

Chinese White or Pale Amber Vinegar

As its name implies, this is a pale-colored rice vinegar that is frequently used in sweet-and-sour dishes and as a dressing for raw vegetables. It is quite a bit sharper than Japanese rice vinegar, and should be used in moderation.

Herb- and Fruit-Flavored Vinegar

Within the last few years, practically every food writer in this country has proclaimed herb vinegars (such as tarragon, basil and rosemary) and fruit vinegars (such as raspberry, strawberry and cherry) to be among the "new ingredients of the eighties." But herb- and fruit-flavored vinegars have been used in America and Europe for hundreds of years.

In the 1800s, raspberry vinegar mixed with seltzer water and a twist of lemon was one of the most popular American summertime drinks. In her 1949 book, *Herbs—Their Culture and Uses*, Rosetta E. Clarkson writes: "Herb vinegars, which are becoming increasingly popular, can be used to flavor ice beverages and culinary dishes and revive flagging spirits. Mint vinegar not only sharpens up a fruit punch but when patted on the forehead will relieve an aching head."

Herb- and fruit-flavored vinegars are made by steeping fresh herbs or fruit in apple cider or wine vinegar. It is a simple and inexpensive process, particularly when the herbs or fruit come out of your own garden. So why are these products so expensive in the stores? Like flavored mustards, they are considered a specialty food item. That means you end up paying for fancy graphics and beautiful bottles.

There are, however, some commercially made herb and fruit vinegars that are superior and well worth their price. What makes the difference in many of these vinegars is the addition of something called an herb or fruit "extract." According to the catalog of Dean & Deluca, one of the finest specialty food shops in Manhattan, "An extract is obtained when fresh fruits or herbs are mixed with vinegar, stored in a large glass container and subjected to hours of slow hydraulic compression. After the appropriate period of seasoning, they are mechanically transformed into a paste. New vinegar is added to dilute the mass, compensate for evaporation and continue the process of seasoning. When the full concentration of flavor is reached, the resulting liquid is filtered and the extract is stored for future use." When the vinegar is ready for bottling, a small amount of extract is added for extra flavoring. Just a few drops of raspberry extract, for example, added to a raspberry-flavored vinegar make a world of difference. Check the label to see if extract has been added; it's a pretty good sign that the vinegar is going to be very fresh tasting.

TASTING NOTES:
Use these herb- and fruit-flavored vinegars with salads, in sweet-and-sour soups and stews, and with mayonnaise and cold vinaigrettes. I tasted dozens of flavored vinegars but found the majority of them to be overpriced and artificial tasting. It makes a lot more sense to make your own flavored vinegars (see recipes on pages 65–70). Listed here are a few products I feel have a really fresh, natural taste.

BEST BRANDS:
Chicama Vineyard's Cranberry Vinegar—Made on the island of Martha's Vineyard, Massachusetts, this vinegar may become a New England tradition. It has the tart, refreshing flavor of cranberries and is delicious in a turkey salad or with a sweet-and-sour cabbage soup. Try simmering cranberries with this vinegar to make a cranberry relish.

[54]

Crabtree & Evelyn's Cherry Red Wine Vinegar—Produced by the "Orléans method" in France, this vinegar is unexpectedly good. (I was sure it would taste like cough medicine!) Made with the addition of cherry extract, it is wonderful with duck or sprinkled over cold artichokes.

Crabtree & Evelyn's Lemon White Wine Vinegar—Produced in the Loire Valley of France, this vinegar has a fresh, clean, lemony flavor. It has bits of lemon floating around in the vinegar that keep its lemon flavor going for a long time. Use as a dip with raw oysters and clams on the half shell, in a lemon mayonnaise and in vinaigrettes.

La Taste Herbes de Provence Vinegar—Although this vinegar is chock-full of a variety of Provençal herbs, it is the powerful flavor of rosemary that comes shining through. It's fantastic with coleslaw, in a garlic-herb mayonnaise or with a cold scallop or lamb salad.

Paul Corcellet Raspberry Vinegar—Made with the addition of raspberry extract, this is a very fresh-tasting fruit vinegar. Although it has a sweet, candy-like smell, its sweetness is subtle and never overpowering. Mix with seltzer water for a refreshing drink or splash on chicken or duck while roasting.

Pommery Raspberry Vinegar—Made by Pommery since 1865, this is a clear vinegar filled with the fragrance and flavor of fresh, ripe Raspberries. Use with pork or duck, in a chicken salad or on top of a mixed fresh fruit salad. Pour some raspberry vinegar over a cored apple or pear and bake; it makes a delicious sweet-and-sour sauce for the fruit.

The Silver Palate Red Wine Basil Vinegar—Made by a Manhattan specialty food shop, this vinegar has a lush maroon color and a fantastically fresh basil flavor. Use on cold pasta salads and with a tomato, mozzarella cheese and basil salad. The Silver Palate also makes a superb *Blueberry Vinegar,* and *Wild Thyme Vinegar.*

Soleillou White Wine Vinegar with Three Fruits—This French-made vinegar is flavored with raspberries, strawberries and bilberries (that's bilberries, not blueberries). It has a clear pink color and a deliciously fresh, fruity flavor.

[55]

Japanese Rice Vinegar (Su)

Japanese rice vinegar is a mild, slightly sweet condiment made from rice wine. It is lighter and more delicate than American and European vinegars with a low acidity of between two to four percent.

Rice vinegar is a key ingredient in Japanese cuisine. The Japanese have a name for dishes made with vinegar, *sunomono*, which literally translated means "vinegared things." These are small salads made up of fruit, vegetables and seafood tossed with a vinegar dressing.

Another popular way of using Japanese rice vinegar is as a seasoning for *sushi* rice—that sticky, sweet rice that is served with thin slices of raw fish. Rice vinegar is used with *sushi* rice because of its gentle tartness and pleasing aftertaste. But the Japanese feel it contributes more than just good taste. In *The Book of Sushi*, Kinjirō Ōmae and Yuzuru Tachibana write: "The observant *sushi* devotee soon notices that, despite the frequency with which they come in contact with water, *sushi* shop workers have soft, smooth hands free of cracks and blemishes. The secret of this soft skin is the mild, protective acidity of [rice] vinegar, one of the most ancient of fermented products."

TASTING NOTES:
The delicate flavor of rice vinegar goes well with all sorts of mild food. It's a terrific vinegar to cook with—especially with chicken, fish and vegetables. Mixed with grated ginger and soy sauce, rice vinegar makes a wonderful dipping sauce. It also goes nicely with avocado and crab-meat salad.

BEST BRANDS:
Daiei Rice Vinegar—This is a good, all-purpose rice vinegar.
Erewhon Sweet Brown Rice Vinegar—The Erewhon natural food company makes this light, refreshing vinegar from glutinous brown rice.

Marukan Seasoned Gourmet Rice Vinegar—This vinegar can be used to make *sushi* rice or as a flavoring ingredient in light, Japanese-style soups, casseroles and stews.

Mitsukan Rice Vinegar—Made in Japan, this is a very delicate, super-light vinegar that is extremely low in acidity—only four percent. Mitsukan also makes an excellent *Sushi-Su Vinegar* that's used to give *sushi* rice its sweet, tart flavor; it's also good with salads and steamed vegetables.

Soken Rice Vinegar (Fujiso)—Delicately flavored, this vinegar goes particularly well with salads and seafood.

Japanese Flavored Vinegars

There are also an endless number of Japanese flavored vinegars. Some of the most common include:

Aji Pon—This delicious rice vinegar is flavored with citrus juice and soy sauce. It tastes more like a seasoned soy sauce than a vinegar; whatever it is, it's fantastic. Use in marinades, with grilled meats and fish, and as a dipping sauce for *sushi* and *sashimi.*

Sushi-Su Vinegar—This sweetened rice vinegar is used to season *sushi* rice. Sushi-Su vinegar is flavored with sugar, corn syrup, salt and M.S.G. Because of the addition of M.S.G. in most commercial brands, many Japanese cooks prefer to mix their own *sushi* vinegar at home.

Tosazu Vinegar—Another sweet vinegar, this one is flavored with bonito (fish) stock, sugar and soy. It has a slightly fishy flavor and is used primarily for *sunomono* and as a condiment sprinkled over fish, vegetable and seaweed dishes.

Ume-Su—This vinegar is made from Japanese plums *(ume)* that are pickled with red *shiso* (beefsteak plant) leaves. It has a beautiful plum color and a slightly salty taste. Use with vegetables, tofu and salads.

[57]

Malt Vinegar

I realized I like malt vinegar when I first ate fish 'n' chips in England. I remember placing my order and, seconds later, being handed a newspaper cone filled with a steaming-hot assortment of fried fish and potatoes. Just as I was about to take the first bite, the lady behind the counter exclaimed, in a thick cockney accent, "Come on, love. You aren't really expecting to eat it without the vinegar now, are you?" She then handed me a bottle of dark-brown liquid. What I remember most about that meal was not the crunchy, delicious flavor of the fried fish and potatoes but the pungent, biting taste of that malt vinegar.

Malt vinegar is made from barley that is mashed, heated with water and then fermented into a crude type of beer, known as "gyle." The "beer" is placed into large vats filled with beech shavings and left to ferment for several weeks, until it turns to vinegar. Then it's filtered and colored with caramel. The varying shades of brown you find in malt vinegars are simply the result of how much caramel has been added.

Malt vinegar has been popular in England since the early sixteenth century. For some reason, it has never really caught on in this country. A few years ago, William Woys Weaver of Paoli, Pennsylvania, wrote a letter to the *Petits Propos Culinaires*, an English culinary journal, on the subject: "Among the wealthy merchant families of Philadelphia, malt vinegar was widely used in the eighteenth and early nineteenth centuries when English tastes and customs were still in vogue here . . . Some people here felt that malt vinegar gave pickles a more characteristic flavor, but even so it has always been considered an English thing."

TASTING NOTES:
- Serve malt vinegar with fish 'n' chips and fried chicken; it seems to cut through the greasiness of fried foods.
- Sprinkle malt vinegar over a potato salad or a cold lamb salad.

[58]

- Malt vinegar adds a delicious flavor to homemade pickles, particularly pickled onions; see recipe on page 226.
- Malt vinegar is the vinegar most often used for making pickled walnuts—a delicious condiment that is a British favorite with roast beef. See page 211 for more information about pickled walnuts.
- Add malt vinegar to barbecue sauces and marinades.

BEST BRANDS:
Chico-San's Malt Vinegar—Chico-San is a natural food company based in Chico, California. According to their catalog, the story behind the vinegar is as follows: "When we met the manufacturer of this product in Japan, we were shown a scroll written approximately 300 years ago, instructing family descendants inheriting the business to adhere to the original formulation for the malt vinegar or pass the plant on to the next inheritor in line." The vinegar has been produced in the same traditional Oriental fashion for over 300 years now. Until recently, the vinegar was produced for domestic use only, but Chico-San persuaded the small Japanese plant to increase their production and Chico-San is now importing it to the United States.

Ellsey's Barley Malt Vinegar—Made in England, this vinegar has a delicious, tart flavor. It's the ultimate accompaniment to fish 'n' chips.

HP Malt Vinegar—This British favorite has a subtle malt flavor.

[59]

Wine Vinegars

Of all the varieties of vinegar sold today, wine vinegars are the most versatile. (For an explanation of how wine vinegar is made, see page 44.)

Wine vinegar breaks down into three major categories: those vinegars made from red and white wine; vinegar made from Spanish sherry wine; and champagne vinegar made from wine produced in France's Champagne region.

Red and White Wine Vinegar

Wine vinegars range in price from about $1 for a weak, "quick method" supermarket brand up to about $25 for a well-aged bottle of "Orléans-style" vinegar. Let me tell you, there is a big difference. A well-made vinegar can transform an ordinary salad into something incredibly good and a poor-quality vinegar can ruin any salad. You don't need to go out and spend $20 to get a really good vinegar. I keep a fairly inexpensive French wine vinegar for everyday use and have a more expensive vinegar on hand for special meals.

Although some people like to store wine vinegar in the refrigerator, it is not necessary. However, vinegars should be kept in a cool, dark place.

TASTING NOTES:
- Wine vinegar goes particularly well in salads. Mix it into a salad of fresh greens, a steamed vegetable salad or homemade coleslaw.
- Add a tablespoon or two of wine vinegar to chicken salad, cold meat salad, shrimp salad or a scallop and orange salad.
- Rub wine vinegar on roasts before cooking; it's particularly good with leg of lamb.
- Add a dash of red wine vinegar to a cold gazpacho or hot vegetable stew.
- Add wine vinegar and chopped shallots to the skillet when sautéing liver, chicken or beef.

- Mix wine vinegar with chopped shallots and use as a dipping sauce for clams and oysters on the half shell.
- Make a marinade with wine vinegar, olive oil, white wine, peppercorns, bay leaves and fresh herbs and use for fish filets or a whole fish. Let the fish marinate for several hours and grill.

BEST BRANDS:
Aunt Bessie's 100% White Riesling Wine Vinegar—This is a unique vinegar made from white Johannisberg Riesling grapes that are grown in Monterey County, California. Aged for over a year by the "Orléans method," it is refreshing and very delicate.

Badia a Coltibuono Red Wine Vinegar—This is a very intense vinegar, almost comparable to an Italian balsamic. When you want the strong, assertive flavor of wine vinegar in a dish, this is an ideal choice. Made from Chianti Classico wines from Tuscany, it is aged in oak barrels for a minimum of three years.

Dessaux Red Wine Vinegar—Made in France, just outside Dijon, this is the vinegar I use every day. It has a tart flavor that seems to blend well with most foods. I particularly like it with salads. Dessaux also makes a *White Wine Tarragon-Flavored Vinegar.*

Gino Failli Vin' Aceto (Red and White Vinegar)—Both of these vinegars have a fantastic, well-rounded flavor. As the label explains: "In Italy the laws specify that only those vinegars deriving from wine fermentation with at least 6% acidity may carry the classification 'aceto.' Vinegars achieving an acidity of over 6% (Failli's is 7½%) are indeed exceptional and are sought after for their exquisite flavor."

Sherry Vinegar

Sherry vinegar is made in the southwestern area of Spain around Jerez. The best sherry vinegars are aged for twenty to thirty years before being bottled.

TASTING NOTES:
- Serve this rich, intensely flavored vinegar with steamed artichokes.
- Add sherry vinegar to seafood and vegetable salads.
- Serve sherry vinegar as a dip for raw fennel.
- Use sherry vinegar to deglaze meat and poultry dishes.
- Make a vinaigrette with sherry vinegar, olive oil, capers and chopped pickles. Serve with cold shrimp, sautéed fish filets and over cold artichoke hearts.
- Marinate spring lamb in sherry vinegar along with a few slivers of garlic. Bake, adding additional vinegar every 30 minutes, to make a pungent, sherry-flavored glaze.
- Use sherry vinegar as a base for potato salad with bits of chopped pear.

BEST BRANDS:
La Posada Spanish Sherry Wine Vinegar—This vinegar has a particularly light sherry wine color and a wonderfully delicate sherry flavor.

Pommery Sherry Vinegar—This is a superb vinegar made from well-aged Spanish sherry. Made by the people who make the world-famous mustard, this sherry vinegar comes in an attractive earthenware bottle.

Romate Sherry Vinegar—Matured in oak casks in the Romate cellars in Jerez, Spain, this is a delicious light sherry vinegar. The sherry flavor lingers on in your mouth even after you've swallowed the vinegar. Try adding a touch of this to a homemade tomato soup. There are two types of Romate vinegar sold in the United

States: *regular* and *V.O.*, which stands for "very old," referring to the fact that it is aged for close to twenty-five years.

Sherry Wine Vinegar—Produced and bottled in Spain by Bodega Paez Moritta, this is a special *reserve* vinegar that is aged for twenty-five years. It has a mellow sherry flavor that is ideal for cooking.

Champagne Wine Vinegar

When you open a bottle of this (rather overpriced) vinegar, don't expect to hear the cork pop. There aren't any bubbles inside. In fact, there isn't even any Champagne.

Champagne vinegar is made from dry white wine produced in the Champagne region of France. That's disappointing, isn't it? Well, it's not all that bad. The fact of the matter is that many champagne wine vinegars are terrific; the dry white wine produced in that part of the world is ideal for making vinegar. You can, however, make your own champagne vinegar by mixing vinegar extract with a bottle of inexpensive champagne. (See page 64 for the recipe.)

TASTING NOTES:
Use champagne wine vinegar as you would any other wine vinegar—in salads, marinades and in soups. It is also a very good cooking vinegar, particularly with chicken.

BEST BRANDS:
Beaufor Champagne Wine Vinegar—Made in Reims, France, this vinegar has been aged in oak and has a mellow flavor.

La Marme Champagne Wine Vinegar—This is absolutely delicious stuff. Made in Reims, France, it has a smooth, refreshing flavor and a silky texture. It's fantastic in salads and with chicken sautéed with garlic.

MAKING YOUR OWN VINEGAR

More and more people are making their own vinegar. It's easy to do but takes some time and patience.

The best idea is to start with a bottle of leftover wine that is free of preservatives; don't use a fortified wine or a wine that has already soured. Simply cover the top of the bottle with a piece of cheesecloth and let it sit in a cool, dark spot for about four months. When you can see a "mother" forming, you'll know the wine is being transformed into vinegar. (See page 44 for an explanation of the "mother" and a description of how wine vinegar is made.) Once the wine has fermented, you can start using the vinegar. Each time you use some of the vinegar, remember to replenish it with additional wine.

BUYING A "MOTHER":

If you like the idea of making your own vinegar but just don't seem to be having any luck developing a "mother," there is another way. A number of wine companies sell vinegar-making kits. These kits contain a "mother" that is guaranteed to start your vinegar and a wooden cask to age the vinegar in. You can choose between a red, white or sherry wine vinegar kit from *Franjoh Cellars* (P. O. Box 7462, Stockton, California 95207), or write to *Wine and The People* (904 University Avenue, Berkeley, California 94710) for information about their vinegar starters.

VINEGAR EXTRACTS:

Another alternative to buying premade vinegar is to buy a *vinegar extract*—a pure, clear, natural concentrate of vinegar. You simply mix 1 cup of extract with 2 cups of liquid (red or white wine, Champagne, port or dry sherry) and flavor with natural fruit extracts or fresh fruits, herbs and seasonings. (See recipe on page 68). Vinegar extracts can be found in specialty food stores; *Surig Essig-Essenz* from West Germany is one of the best brands.

MAKING YOUR OWN FLAVORED VINEGAR

The beauty of making your own flavored vinegar at home is that you can experiment and create your own combinations. You can use any mixture of fresh herbs, fresh fruit, spices, garlic, shallots, and fruit and herb extracts (extracts are available at health food stores). See the list of possible combinations on page 70.)

Master Recipe for Homemade Flavored Vinegar

Making flavored vinegar is extremely easy. The only requirement is that the herbs or fruit you use be *very fresh*. These vinegars make wonderful gifts—make them in the summer when everything is ripe and fresh and then give them as Christmas gifts. The basic "recipe" is as follows:

1. Choose an attractive bottle. It can be an old wine, Champagne, or imported beer bottle or mason jar. Wash and rinse in boiling water and dry thoroughly.
2. In a stainless-steel saucepan, heat enough apple cider, red, white or sherry wine vinegar to fill the bottle. Heat it over a low heat without letting it boil; you simply want to warm it up.
3. When making an herb-flavored vinegar, use about 1 cup of fresh herbs to 2 cups of vinegar—it really depends on the strength of the herbs you choose. (The herbs can be on or off the stem.) For fruit-flavored vinegars, use about 1 cup of fresh fruit to 1 cup of vinegar. Clean the herbs or fruit, and place in the bottle. Cover with the warm vinegar and let cool before sealing.
4. Place the vinegar in a cool, dark spot for about ten days to two weeks before tasting. Once you can really taste the herb or fruit

flavor then the vinegar is ready; if the vinegar is still weak, let it sit for another few days.

5. At this point, you can either leave the herbs and fruit in the bottle or strain the vinegar through a piece of cheesecloth and discard the herbs or fruit. Then put the vinegar back in the bottle.

Strawberry and Pepper Champagne Wine Vinegar

Strawberries and Champagne are such a natural match that I decided to try them together in a vinegar. The ripe strawberries and the peppercorns permeate the champagne wine vinegar and leave a fresh strawberry flavor, with just a subtle hint of pepper. The strawberry-colored vinegar that results is exquisite. Use this vinegar with green salads, fruit salads, served over broiled chicken and on mild types of fish, such as filet of sole.

    1 cup ripe strawberries, thinly sliced
    6 whole, black peppercorns
    1 cup champagne wine vinegar, or a good dry white
      wine vinegar

Place the berries and peppercorns into a clear bottle or mason jar and cover with the vinegar. Seal the jar tightly and let sit for about two weeks. The vinegar should turn a reddish-pink color and have the taste and smell of fresh strawberries. Strain the vinegar through a piece of cheesecloth and discard the strawberries. Pour the vinegar into a clean bottle or jar and seal. Use within two months. *Makes 1 cup.*

Bill Bell's Red and Green Chile Pepper Vinegar

This recipe was given to me by Bill Bell, a good friend from Portsmouth, New Hampshire. Long, thin red and green chile peppers are stuffed into a clean wine bottle and then covered with a good apple cider vinegar; the result is a wonderful-tasting and beautiful-looking vinegar.

This vinegar is delicious sprinkled over salads, fried eggs, and in potato salad. As you use the vinegar, you should replenish it with additional apple cider vinegar.

> About 1½ pounds red and green chile peppers
> Whole-apple cider vinegar

Wash the peppers and let dry. Fill a clean, clear wine bottle with the peppers until they come to the top of the bottle. Fill the bottle with the vinegar and cork. Let stand for 24 hours before using.

Champagne Tarragon Vinegar

You can make a fantastic vinegar using a vinegar extract (see page 64 for an explanation), Champagne and fresh herbs. There's no point using a really expensive Champagne for this vinegar—any dry, bubbly Champagne will do. Try simmering chicken in a cup of this vinegar, along with a cup of Champagne and a few cloves of fresh garlic. It's also delicious sprinkled over a mixed green salad.

    1 cup vinegar extract
    2 cups Champagne, or dry white wine
    2 to 3 cups fresh tarragon, or any other fresh herb
    2 cloves peeled garlic

In a large, stainless-steel saucepan, simmer the extract and Champagne over a moderate heat until warm, about 5 minutes.

Place the herbs and garlic into sterilized jars and cover with the warm vinegar mixture. Let cool and seal tightly. Let sit in a cool, dark spot for 10 days before using. *Makes 3 cups.*

Homemade Apple Cider Vinegar

Making your own apple cider vinegar is incredibly easy. Start with a good, pure apple cider; that means no preservatives or additives. Simply strain the cider through a triple layer of cheesecloth or a clean tea towel (in order to remove any sediment) into a large crock or dark-colored glass bottle. (You can also use a plain glass jar and wrap it in tin foil to keep out the light.) Fill the bottle about ¾ of the way and cover with a triple layer of cheesecloth; this allows the air to get in, but keeps out dust and bugs.

Let the cider ferment in a cool, dark spot for about four months. (If you feel impatient and want more immediate results, add about ½ cup good apple cider vinegar or dry white wine to speed up the fermentation process.) After three to four months, check the vinegar. It should have a clear, cider color and a large, gelatinous "mother" floating on the top. If it tastes strong and vinegary, it's ready to use; if it still tastes weak, let it sit for another few weeks. Carefully strain the vinegar through a triple layer of cheesecloth and place into clean bottles. If you feel that the vinegar is too strong, simply dilute it with a bit of water. Add a fresh batch of cider to the "mother" and repeat.

Ginger-Apple Vinegar

Slivers of fresh ginger give apple cider vinegar a refreshing (and slightly peppery) flavor. Use with steamed fish, on salads and with stir-fried vegetables.

    1 three-inch piece of fresh ginger
    1 cup whole apple cider vinegar
    1 teaspoon sugar

Peel the ginger and slice into five thin pieces. Using a sharp knife, score an X into each piece. Place the ginger into a small, clean jar and add the vinegar and sugar. Cover the jar and let sit for 10 days. Strain the vinegar and discard the ginger. Clean out the jar and add the vinegar. Use sparingly. *Makes 1 cup.*

Favorite Flavored Vinegar Combinations

- White wine vinegar with rosemary and orange rind
- White wine vinegar with tarragon and lemon balm
- Red wine vinegar with opal basil and garlic
- White wine vinegar with crushed dill, celery, coriander, cumin and caraway seeds
- Apple cider vinegar with mint and a touch of sugar
- Apple cider vinegar with fresh dill and dill seed
- White wine vinegar with orange slices and orange extract
- White wine vinegar with fresh raspberries
- Red wine vinegar with fresh blueberries
- Japanese rice wine vinegar with ginger
- Cider vinegar with chile peppers and garlic
- Lemon-flavored white wine vinegar with garlic, shallots and orange rind
- Champagne vinegar with raspberry extract and fresh raspberries

COOKING WITH VINEGAR

Japanese-Style Marinated Mushrooms

½ cup thinly sliced scallions
1 small sweet red pepper, finely chopped
1 small green hot chile pepper, finely chopped
½ cup *mirin* (sweet Japanese rice wine)
½ cup Japanese or light soy sauce
½ cup olive oil
4 tablespoons minced fresh ginger
3 tablespoons Italian balsamic vinegar
2 tablespoons Japanese rice wine vinegar
1½ tablespoons sesame oil
¼ teaspoon freshly ground pepper
1½ pounds small mushrooms, cleaned with stems intact

Mix all the ingredients except the mushrooms and taste for seasoning. If marinade tastes too oily, add additional rice wine vinegar; if it's too tart and vinegary, add additional oil and soy sauce. Mix in the mushrooms and let marinate for at least 1 hour. Serve at room temperature or cold. *Serves 4 to 6.*

Chicken with Garlic in a Vinegar Sauce

This is a simple dish that can be made in under an hour. You can use any type of vinegar you want with this recipe—raspberry, red wine or sherry vinegar works particularly well. The vinegar adds a terrific, pungent flavor to the chicken and the 20 cloves of garlic add a surprisingly subtle flavor.

             1 tablespoon butter
             1 tablespoon virgin olive oil
             1 three-pound chicken, cut into serving pieces
          1½ teaspoons dried tarragon, or 1 teaspoon fresh
                Salt and freshly ground black pepper
           20 whole cloves garlic, peeled
             3 cups sliced mushrooms
           ¾ cup vinegar, see note above
          1½ cups chicken broth, preferably homemade

In a large skillet or a casserole, melt the butter with oil over a high heat until hot. Brown the chicken on both sides and sprinkle with the tarragon and salt and pepper to taste. Remove the chicken to a plate. Add the garlic and mushrooms to the hot skillet and sauté for about 2 minutes, or until lightly browned. Add the vinegar and let boil for about 2 minutes. Add the chicken broth and bring the sauce to a boil.

Place the chicken back into the skillet, reduce the heat to moderately high, and let the chicken simmer, covered, for about 40 minutes, or until cooked. (To test the chicken, place a fork or sharp knife into the skin; the juices should be yellow and not pink.) Place the chicken onto a serving platter and cover with the sauce. Serve with rice. *Serves 4.*

Strawberries, Oranges and Black Olives in a Balsamic Vinegar Dressing

The idea for this refreshing salad came from Ernie Brown Goldman, an actress who lives in San Francisco. This unlikely combination is delicious; if you like, you can add walnut halves instead of black olives.

    1 cup thinly sliced ripe strawberries
    3 tablespoons balsamic vinegar
    1 teaspoon sugar
    2 oranges, peeled and thinly sliced
    ½ cup black Italian or Greek olives (or walnut halves)

Place the strawberries in a bowl with the vinegar and sugar and let marinate at room temperature for about 30 minutes.

Arrange the orange slices on a serving plate or bowl and spoon the berries, without the vinegar, on top. Scatter the olives (or walnuts) on top and then pour the vinegar over the salad. Serve cold. *Serves 2.*

Bean Sprout, Avocado,
Water Chestnut and Walnut Salad with
Chinese Red Vinegar Dressing

1 clove garlic, minced
1 tablespoon minced ginger
3 tablespoons Chinese red rice vinegar
5 tablespoons flavored grapeseed oil or peanut oil
   Salt and pepper to taste
1½ cups assorted bean sprouts
6 fresh water chestnuts, peeled and thinly sliced
1 avocado, thinly sliced
¼ cup walnut halves
½ small red onion, thinly sliced

In a salad bowl, mix the garlic and ginger. Whisk in the vinegar, oil, salt and pepper. Add the bean sprouts to the middle of the bowl and arrange the water chestnuts, avocado slices, walnuts and onions around them. Serve immediately. *Serves 2 to 4.*

Sweet-and-Sour Red Cabbage Soup

Balsamic vinegar is what gives this delicious soup its pungent flavor. It was created by Sara Moulton, *chef tournant* at La Tulipe restaurant in New York City. The soup may be served hot or cold, but if served cold the bacon should be discarded after the fat is rendered. (This recipe first appeared in *The Cook's Magazine*.)

        4 slices bacon, diced
        4 medium leeks, finely diced
     1½ teaspoons allspice
        ½ teaspoon ground cloves
     2½ teaspoons minced garlic
        4 packed tablespoons brown sugar
        ½ cup balsamic vinegar
        1 small red cabbage, shredded (about 4 cups)
        2 14-ounce cans Italian plum tomatoes, finely chopped
            (with juice)
        5 cups chicken stock, preferably homemade
            Salt and freshly ground black pepper to taste

        THE GARNISH
        1 cup sour cream
            Freshly chopped dill or chives

In a stainless-steel pot, sauté the bacon until all the fat is rendered and the bacon is golden, about 10 minutes. Add the leeks and cook over low heat, covered, for about 15 minutes, or until soft. Stir in the allspice, cloves and garlic and cook for 2 minutes. Add the brown sugar and vinegar and stir until the sugar is dissolved, about 3 to 4 minutes. Add the cabbage and tomatoes and cook, covered, over low heat for 30 minutes, stirring occasionally.

Add the chicken stock and bring the soup to a boil. Simmer, uncovered, for 30 minutes. Add salt and pepper to taste and serve with sour cream and chopped dill or chives on top. *Serves 6.*

Avocado with Japanese Rice Vinegar and Sesame Seeds

The mild, creamy flavor of avocado lends itself to the subtle sweetness of rice vinegar. This makes a delicious appetizer or a salad served with grilled fish.

    2 tablespoons Japanese rice vinegar
    ½ teaspoon Japanese or light soy sauce
    ½ teaspoon lemon juice
    ½ teaspoon sesame seeds
    1 ripe avocado, thinly sliced
    ½ teaspoon bonito (dried fish) flakes (optional)

In a small bowl, mix the vinegar, soy sauce, lemon juice and sesame seeds. Arrange the avocado slices on a serving plate, overlapping them slightly. Spoon the sauce over the avocado and sprinkle with bonito flakes, if desired. *Serves 1 to 2.*

Oriental-Style Beef with Two Vinegars and Sesame Oil Marinade

    1   pound lean flank steak
    1½ tablespoons sherry wine vinegar
    1½ tablespoons red wine vinegar
    3   tablespoons soy sauce
    1   tablespoon cornstarch (optional)
    1   tablespoon tahini (ground sesame paste)
    2   tablespoons minced garlic
    2   tablespoons minced fresh ginger
    1   small onion, thinly sliced
    2   tablespoons sesame oil
    2   tablespoons peanut or vegetable oil
    4   scallions, cut into 2½-inch pieces

Place the meat in the freezer for 15 minutes; remove and slice on the diagonal as thinly as possible. In a large bowl, whisk together the sherry and red wine vinegars, soy sauce, cornstarch, tahini, 1 tablespoon of the garlic, 1 tablespoon of the ginger, the onion and 1 tablespoon of the sesame oil. Add the meat and let marinate, uncovered, for 2 to 4 hours at room temperature.

In a wok or large skillet, heat the peanut or vegetable oil over a high heat until hot. Add the remaining tablespoon of sesame oil and the remaining tablespoon of ginger and garlic. Let cook for about 5 seconds, and then add the meat slices along with the marinade. Add the scallions and stir quickly; let cook for about 4 to 5 minutes or until the meat is tender. If the mixture begins to dry out, add additional soy sauce. Serve hot with steamed rice and orange slices. *Serves 2.*

Coleslaw with Walnuts and Raisins

Vinegar and cabbage work together beautifully. This coleslaw is full of good flavors and textures, but it is the addition of vinegar that makes it really delicious.

          3 cups grated red and white cabbage
          ½ cup chopped walnut halves
          ½ cup raisins
        1½ tablespoons grainy or Dijon mustard
          ½ cup red wine vinegar
          2 tablespoons balsamic vinegar (optional)
          2 tablespoons olive oil
          ¾ to 1 cup mayonnaise, preferably homemade
    (see page 161)
          ¼ cup milk
             Salt and freshly ground black pepper to taste

Place the cabbage, walnuts and raisins in a large salad bowl and toss. Mix in the mustard and then the vinegar(s), oil, ¾ cup of the mayonnaise and the milk. Add salt and pepper to taste. If you like your coleslaw creamier, add the additional ¼ cup of mayonnaise. Serve at room temperature or chilled. *Serves about 6.*

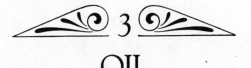

3

OIL

Oil is a lot like wine. If it is well made, it will have the true taste and aroma of the raw ingredients that went into it. If it is poorly made, it can be bitter and harsh or simply bland and tasteless.

To many people, oil is just a utilitarian product used for cooking food and greasing pans. Most of the oils sold in this country are so highly refined and deodorized that they aren't capable of doing much more. But there are also pure, unrefined oils—oils that have color, fragrance and a luscious, sensual taste.

Consider the rich aroma and nutty flavor of hazelnuts, almonds and walnuts; the luscious, fruity taste of the olive; the light, pure, nutty essence of peanuts; and the flavor of lightly toasted sesame seeds. These are characteristics of pure, unrefined oils that compliment and enhance food. They are oils that deserve to be called condiments and are best appreciated at room temperature, straight from the bottle—sprinkled over salads, vegetables, fish and meat. Of course, you can also cook with these oils but, in many cases, their distinctive flavor is lost when heated.

OIL
SURVEY

Pure oils should have a good color, a distinctive fragrance and fresh taste.

Listed below are descriptions of the major varieties of oils that can be used as condiments. I've also given specific recommendations for those brands that I consider to be superior, along with some ideas for how to use them. There's also a section on flavored oils that will tell you which ones are worth the price and how to make your own at home.

Olive Oil

I have a friend who spends $25 for a bottle of Italian extra virgin olive oil every few months. She isn't particularly wealthy. She isn't even an outstanding cook. But she loves olive oil and appreciates the difference between a cheap olive oil and a more expensive, first-pressing, extra virgin. Some might say she's a fanatic. I think she's smart. A really good olive oil is capable of transforming everyday food into an extraordinary taste experience.

Choosing a good olive oil has become complicated. And when you're spending $25 for a bottle of oil, you want to make sure you're getting something special. One way to protect your investment is by reading and understanding the label.

The first thing you'll notice is the grading: "Virgin," "Extra Virgin," "First Pressing," "Cold Pressing," et cetera. Don't panic. It's not nearly as complicated as it sounds.

Olives are pressed for oil three times. The first pressing is called *Extra Virgin*. It is the purest oil and the most expensive.

Extra virgin oil is made from the choicest olives. The fruit is handpicked and the oil is extracted manually by cold stone presses. (No heat is used when making extra virgin olive oil; although a hot press can extract additional oil from the olive, this oil is of poorer quality.) The sediment is then filtered out of most oils; some producers, however, believe that the sediment contains a rich, olive flavor that should be left in. (If you notice that your oil is cloudy with bits of sediment floating around the bottom of the bottle, there's no cause for alarm. It's further evidence that you've got the real thing.) Extra virgin olive oil is prized for its low acidity; to be labeled "extra virgin," the oil can have no more than one percent acid.

The second pressing of the olives is done with high pressure and with the addition of heat. These oils are labeled *Virgin Olive Oil*, *Superfine Olive Oil* and *Fine Olive Oil*. All these names refer to the same grade of oil. These oils have a higher degree of acidity, about 1.5 to 5 percent.

The third pressing of oil is called *Pure Olive Oil*. Made from second and third "hot pressings," this is the least expensive type of olive oil you can buy. Pure olive oil is usually made from lower quality olives or the pulp left over from the first two pressings. It is generally mixed with a higher grade olive oil to give it a better flavor. The word "Pure" on the label simply refers to the fact that no other types of oil have been added.

TASTING NOTES:
The four major olive-oil-producing countries are Italy, France, Greece and Spain. *Italian olive oil* is considered by many people to be the finest in the world—particularly those oils produced in the Tuscany, Liguria and Umbria regions. These oils are very rich (some say heavy) with a full olive flavor and a deep, almost emerald-green color. *French olive oil* is more delicate. It's known for its sweet, fruity flavor and a light, golden-yellow color. Many people feel that the olives grown in Provence, in southeastern France, make the most delicate and fruity oil in the world. *Spanish olive oil*

has a strong, assertive olive flavor with a thick consistency. *Greek olive oil* is also thick but has a lighter olive flavor. The Spanish and Greek oils are generally less expensive than the Italian and French.

In the last few years, there have been a growing number of *American olive oils*, produced primarily in California. In general, these oils are excellent. They range from rich, olivey, Italian-style oils to more delicate French-style oils. Since most of these oils are produced on a small scale, the prices tend to be high.

Each type of olive oil has its own purpose. Just because extra virgin oil is considered the best doesn't mean it's right for every dish.

Extra virgin olive oils should be treated with respect. You're wasting your money if you use them in complex sauces and recipes that call for dozens of ingredients. They are best served room temperature because high heat can destroy their delicate flavor.

These are just a few of my favorite ways to use olive oil:

- There is nothing better than an extra virgin olive oil mixed with a well-aged wine vinegar sprinkled over a salad—be it made of assorted greens, cold seafood, lightly steamed vegetables, chicken or meat.
- Use extra virgin olive oil for making pesto sauce.
- Homemade mayonnaise and flavored mayonnaise are particularly rich and flavorful when made with olive oil; see recipes on pages 161–63.
- Make a dipping sauce with extra virgin olive oil flavored with equal parts coarse sea salt and coarsely chopped black pepper and serve with raw fennel and other raw vegetables.
- Spoon a tablespoon of olive oil onto a thick chunk of Italian bread and top with paper-thin slices of prosciutto and a few grindings of black pepper.
- Use virgin and pure oils for making sauces, stews, sautéed vegetables, stir-fries, roasts and pasta sauces.
- Heat 2 tablespoons of virgin olive oil over a high heat. Add sliced wild mushrooms, fiddlehead ferns or thinly sliced zucchini and sauté for a few minutes. Add 2 cloves of chopped garlic and some

chopped fresh herbs and sauté another minute or two, until the vegetables begin to turn golden brown and tender. Serve immediately.

- Heat 2½ tablespoons of virgin olive oil over high heat. Add a tin of anchovies, 2 cloves of garlic, 2 tablespoons chopped parsley and 5 chopped pimientos and let cook down. Serve on top of pasta or steamed spinach.

BEST BRANDS:

Extra Virgin Olive Oils

Antinori Extra Virgin Olive Oil—The Antinori family has been famous for their full-flavored Tuscan wines for over 600 years. They have also been making an equally superb olive oil for years but, until recently, it was only sold locally. This delicate, fruity oil is now being sold in the United States. It is expensive, but it's well worth the price.

Badia a Coltibuono Extra Virgin Olive Oil—Made in Tuscany, this oil has a full, rich olive flavor without being heavy or greasy. It's delicious on salads and in cold pasta sauces.

Balducci's Extra Virgin Olive Oil—Balducci's, which is one of Manhattan's most successful specialty food shops, purchased an entire pressing of olive oil from a small estate in Tuscany and is now bottling it under their own name. The oil has a rich, greenish-gold color and an appealing, fruity, flowery taste.

Castello di Cacchiano Extra Virgin Olive Oil—Made in Tuscany in the Chianti Classico wine region, this oil has a delicate, slightly fruity flavor. It is superb. You may find some sediment at the bottom of the bottle; the oil has not been filtered in order to retain all of its pure olive flavor.

Crabtree & Evelyn First Pressing, Cold Pressed Olive Oil—Made in France by Roger Michel, this delicate, deliciously light oil is made from tiny ripe olives grown in Nice.

Emilio Pucci Extra Virgin Olive Oil—As much as I hate the idea of "designer food," this oil, produced by the Marchese Emilio Pucci, is excellent. Produced on the Pucci estate near Florence, it has a beautiful emerald-green color and the fresh, lush taste of Tuscan olives.

Goya Extra Virgin Olive Oil—Goya is the number-one importer and seller of Spanish extra virgin olive oil in the United States. This award-winning oil is thick and silky with a rich, pronounced olive flavor.

Hilaire Fabre Père & Fils Extra Virgin Olive Oil—This is a very light, delicately flavored oil from France.

Kimberly California Olive Oil—Buying this oil is a little like buying fine California wine; the bottle is similar, the vintage date is listed on the label, and the liquid inside is fruity and full flavored. The oil is cold-pressed from ripened Mission olives grown in northern California.

La Taste Olive Oil—I think this is one of the best olive oils I've ever tasted. Made in Vallée des Baux in Provence, it has a very delicate fruity flavor with a subtle hint of pepper.

Old Monk Extra Virgin Olive Oil—Old Monk disappeared from the American market for a while but, happily, it is back. Made in Nice, it has an unusually light, fruity flavor and a beautiful golden color.

Poggio al Sole Extra Virgin Olive Oil—Produced in the Chianti Classico wine region of Tuscany, this deep-green oil has an earthy, fresh flavor.

Roselle Extra Virgin Olive Oil—Made in Tuscany, this first, cold-pressed oil has a spectacular emerald-green color and a rich, fruity taste.

Sciabica's 100% Pure Virgin Natural Olive Oil—The Sciabica family has been producing olive oil in northern California since 1936. Nick Sciabica originally worked in an olive oil mill in Sicily around the turn of the century; his son started the business in California and now his grandson, Daniel, is following in his footsteps. The Sciabicas make a thick, delicious oil from California's own Mission olives.

Siurana Extra Virgin Olive Oil—This Spanish olive oil is strongly flavored and fruity. It also happens to be very moderately priced.

Virgin and Pure Olive Oils

Amastra Pure Olive Oil—I love this oil for everyday use. It has a wonderful olive flavor that enhances, rather than overwhelms food. Made in Castelvetrano, Sicily, it is moderately priced. I buy it by the gallon, which makes it even less expensive.

Bertolli Pure Olive Oil—This is a factory-made olive oil that is an Italian favorite. For me it has practically no olive flavor, but is reasonably priced and good for cooking.

Crinos Pure Olive Oil—Made from Calamata olives, this Greek oil is a good buy. It has a golden color and a mild olive flavor that makes it an ideal cooking oil.

Nut Oils

Oils extracted from nuts are fairly new in this country but they have been popular in Europe for a long time. A lot of people consider these oils to be an unnecessary extravagance. But if you've ever tasted a salad of Italian *radicchio* lettuce sprinkled with walnut oil, or filet of sole drizzled with almond oil, then you know these oils are worth it. Granted, they are expensive, but a little bit of their rich, nutty flavor goes a long way.

Essentially, these oils are made by crushing nuts—almonds, walnuts or hazelnuts—and then heating them until they turn to a thick golden-brown paste. The paste is then subjected to hydraulic pressure to squeeze out every possible ounce of oil.

Almond Oil

TASTING NOTES:
Almond oil has a delicate, fresh almond flavor and a beautiful amber color. It is delicious in vinaigrettes accompanied by slivered almonds. Instead of butter, try heating a few teaspoons of almond oil and pouring it over freshly steamed green beans or broccoli. Almond oil is particularly good with artichokes; melt a tablespoon of butter and add a tablespoon of almond oil and use as a dip for hot or cold artichokes.

BEST BRANDS:
Huilerie du Berry Almond Oil—The Guenard family has been producing nut oils in the Loire Valley of France since 1824. Almond is their newest oil; it is exceptional because it tastes like fresh, roasted almonds and not almond extract.
Pommery Pure Almond Oil—This is a delicious oil—rich and full of pure almond flavor.

Hazelnut Oil

Hazelnut oil is fairly new in the United States but has long been popular in France, where it is made. This oil has the delicate scent of fresh hazelnuts and a wonderful toasted hazelnut flavor.

TASTING NOTES:
Use hazelnut oil in vinaigrettes, sauces and added to homemade mayonnaise. It's delicious on broiled fish; see recipe on page 97. Try lining a cookie or cake tin with hazelnut oil; it will give a wonderful hazelnut flavor to whatever you are baking.

BEST BRANDS:
Huilerie du Berry Hazelnut Oil—Made in the Loire Valley by the Guenard family, this is a superb, richly flavored oil.
Pommery Pure Hazelnut Oil—This oil is rich and nutty; it's fantastic on salads.
Vivier Hazelnut Oil—This oil has a fresh, pure taste; it's delicious on salads and added to cookies.

Walnut Oil

Walnut oil is made in the Périgord and Burgundy regions of France. Unlike other nut oils, walnut oil is made from nuts that are dried and then cold-pressed. The walnut, which contains 60 percent oil, produces a light, delicate oil.

TASTING NOTES:
Walnut oil is terrific on salads, particularly when you combine it with bits of walnuts. Add walnut oil to a chicken or turkey salad along with some grapes and chopped walnuts. Brush a thin coat of walnut oil on grilled fish and steaks just before serving.

BEST BRANDS:
Crabtree & Evelyn's Walnut Oil—This oil has a pure, nutty flavor that enhances food beautifully.
Dauphi-Noix Walnut Oil—This is a delicately flavored walnut oil that is particularly good on mixed green salads.
Pommery Walnut Oil—This oil is filled with the luscious flavor and aroma of toasted walnuts.

Sesame Oil

Take a whiff of this oil before you use it. Once you smell the rich, intense scent of toasted sesame seeds, you'll realize just how strong this oil is. A few drops of sesame oil can add an outrageously good flavor to many foods.

Sesame oil, which is extracted from sesame seeds, is a key ingredient in Oriental cuisine. It's primarily used for cooking (almost always in combination with other, milder oils), but it is also used as a condiment—to flavor simply prepared foods and cold salads.

There are various types of sesame oil. The thicker, browner oils, which are produced in Japan and China, have the fullest, richest flavor. The oils from the Middle East are lighter and far less aromatic.

Many health food stores sell their own brand of sesame oil. Some of them are good, but they are generally very light and almost too subtle. The best sesame oils can be found in Oriental supermarkets.

TASTING NOTES:
- A few drops of sesame oil is delicious with scrambled eggs; aside from adding flavor, sesame oil can be used, instead of butter, to keep the eggs from sticking to the pan—see recipe on page 102.
- Sesame oil adds great flavor to mild soups and stews. Add a few drops to each bowl just before serving.
- Chicken livers with thinly sliced cucumbers stir-fried in sesame oil is delicious; the nutty flavor of the oil complements the flavor of the liver beautifully.
- Sesame oil mixed with a few tablespoons of peanut oil, soy sauce, grated ginger and sliced hot chile peppers makes a great dipping sauce for seafood and chicken.
- One of my favorite ways to use sesame oil is to heat it with a touch of Chinese peanut oil and pour it over steamed or pan-fried fish just before serving. The hot oil sizzles the fish's skin and seeps through to flavor the flesh.

- Add sesame oil to a cold squid or lobster salad.
- Sauté green beans, artichoke hearts or thinly sliced cucumbers in sesame oil and garnish with chopped sweet red pepper.

BEST BRANDS:
Dynasty Sesame Oil—This Chinese oil has a fresh, pure taste. Add a few drops to stir-fried vegetables or a homemade mayonnaise.

Ho-Tai Sesame Oil—This "100 percent pure" sesame oil has a potent sesame flavor that won't overwhelm food the way some of the stronger Oriental oils do. It's produced by the Tienley Company in Japan.

Kadoya 100% Pure Sesame Oil—Made in Japan, this oil is now available in many supermarkets across the country. It has a good, pure sesame flavor.

Kimland Brand Pure Sesame Oil—Made in Taiwan, this is a very dark, intense oil.

Mese Hsin Tung Yuan Black Sesame Oil—Made from black sesame seeds, this pure oil is rich and very flavorful.

Roland Top Grade Sesame Oil—This Japanese oil has a dark-brown color and a rich, intense flavor; a little bit goes a long way.

Walnut Acres Unrefined Sesame Oil—Made by Walnut Acres, a natural foods company in Penns Creek, Pennsylvania, this is an extremely light, delicate oil that is not nearly as potent as the Oriental varieties. It's particularly good in salads and cold sauces.

Peanut (or Groundnut) Oil

First, a little-known fact. The peanut is actually not a nut, but a seed of the pea family. When pea pods form, they turn down and bury themselves in the ground, which is why peanuts are also called groundnuts.

Peanuts contain about 50 percent oil. When they are cold-pressed, the oil that is extracted is pure and full of rich peanut flavor. Unfortunately, most American peanut oils are so refined that they have virtually no peanut taste. They make excellent cooking oils but shouldn't be relied on for adding flavor to foods. However, in parts of France and Asia, peanut oil is a pure, unrefined oil that is prized for its distinctive peanut flavor and nutty fragrance. These oils are generally more expensive than the refined American peanut oils, but they are definitely worth the extra expense.

TASTING NOTES:
- Because of its high smoking point, peanut oil is most frequently used as a frying oil. Use it to fry tempura, chicken, fish filets or vegetables.
- Try heating a teaspoon or two of peanut oil with a touch of sesame oil and pouring it over steamed or stir-fried spinach or lettuce.
- Chinese peanut oil mixed with grated ginger, thinly sliced scallions and coarse sea salt makes a fantastic dipping sauce for steamed or boiled chicken.
- Mix peanut oil, soy sauce, minced garlic, grated ginger and scallions and serve as a dipping sauce for shrimp or crab.
- Make a vinaigrette using peanut oil, sesame oil, grapefruit juice and wine vinegar. Toss with poached scallops and watercress and serve cold.

BEST BRANDS:

Chinese Peanut Oil—Imported from China, you can buy this pure peanut oil in plastic bottles by the gallon. The label is written entirely in Chinese and the "logo" is the Chinese symbol for happiness. This oil has just recently been imported to the United States and it is as good a peanut oil as you can hope to find anywhere. The following Chinese peanut oils are also available by the gallon; they are all pure and well flavored: *Gold Key Pure Peanut Oil* from China; *Hop Hing Peanut Oil* from Hong Kong; *Knife Brand Pure Groundnut Oil*; and *Red Lantern Brand Chinese Peanut Oil*.

Dauphi-Noix Peanut Oil—This pure French peanut oil has a delicious peanut flavor and a very subtle, nutty scent.

Huilor Pure Peanut Oil—Made in France, this is a delicious, light oil.

Walnut Acres Virgin Peanut Oil—This oil, made by a natural foods company in Penns Creek, Pennsylvania, has a subtle peanut flavor.

Flavored Oil

Oils flavored with fresh herbs, chile peppers, garlic and spices are hot items in specialty food shops these days. While a number of these products are terrific, many are overpriced. You can make your own flavored oils at home for a lot less; see pages 94–97 for recipes.

TASTING NOTES:
- Use flavored oils in vinaigrettes along with fresh herbs.
- Pour flavored oils on cold pasta and vegetable salads.
- Try making a marinade for beef or chicken using flavored oils, vinegar, red wine and fresh herbs.
- Add a few tablespoons of herb-flavored oils to a homemade mayonnaise (see pages 162–63).
- Brush these oils onto fish, chicken, steaks and shish kebab before broiling or barbecuing.
- Use flavored grapeseed oils for cooking beef fondue.
- Use a basil- or mixed-herb-flavored oil as the base of a pesto sauce.

BEST BRANDS:
Listed below are a few brands of flavored oils that are definitely worth their price. They have a pure, fresh flavor that is hard to duplicate, even when you're making your own using the very freshest ingredients.

Crabtree & Evelyn Blended Olive Oil and Grapeseed Oil—This French oil, which is 60 percent olive and 40 percent grapeseed, is flavored with wild thyme, fresh bay leaves, rosemary, savory and pepper. It has a fresh herb flavor with a delicious peppery bite. Use with broiled meats, shish kebab, in paella and salads.

The Silver Palate Basil Oil—This golden-colored oil has a wonderful fresh basil flavor; it is delicious on pasta and in salads. Use with pesto sauces and in a basil-flavored mayonnaise. Pour a little of this oil over a salad of thinly sliced ripe tomatoes, slices of smoked mozzarella and fresh, chopped basil leaves.

Soleillou Grapeseed Oils—"Soleillou"—the French word for "the little sun"—is a small company located in sunny Provence that makes terrific herb-flavored grapeseed oils. (Grapeseed oil is a light, aromatic oil that is a by-product of the wine industry.) Their oils come in three flavor variations: *Natural Herb Flavored Provence Grape Seed Oil* is flavored with tarragon, thyme, basil, coarse black pepper and sea salt. It is peppery and full of fresh herb flavors. Be sure to shake the bottle well before using so that all the bits of fresh herbs and pepper don't stay stuck to the bottom of the bottle. Try drizzling a bit onto clams or oysters on the half shell and then broiling them for a minute. *Provence Herb Flavored Oil for Fish* is filled with bits of fennel, thyme, bay (laurel) leaves and cumin seeds. It is delicious on broiled fish or as a marinade for seafood and meat. *Provence Herb Flavored Oil for Broiling Meat* is flavored with rosemary, wild thyme, basil, fennel, garlic, pepper and sea salt. It is not as potent as the other oils, but is delicious with grilled meats and sautéed vegetables.

S & B La Yu Chilli Oil—This stuff is dynamite. It is a red-hot, chile-pepper-flavored sesame oil. It's fantastic over cold Chinese noodles, in dipping sauces and brushed over grilled foods. Use sparingly.

Spice Oil—Made in Japan and distributed by the Daiei Trading Co., there are three varieties of these spiced vegetable oils: *Beefsteak Plant Leaves* gives one of these oils a slightly spicy, smokey flavor; use it with salads and on shredded vegetables. There is also a *Lemon-Lime Flavored Oil* that is used to season meats and fish and a *Ginger-Spiced Oil* that adds good flavor to grilled seafood, meats and vegetable dishes.

Roland Chili Oil—The dragons on the label of this chile-pepper-flavored peanut oil aren't just an insignificant graphic device; this stuff is fiery hot. Made in Taiwan, it will add peppery flavor to Chinese dishes or cold noodles, marinades or barbecues.

MAKING YOUR OWN
FLAVORED OIL

It makes a lot of sense to make your own flavored oils. For one thing, it's generally much less expensive than buying the commercially produced oils; but the real fun of making them at home is that you can create your own combinations.

On the following pages, you'll find recipes for making herb-flavored oils and hot chile oil. I've also included a list of my favorite flavored-oil combinations. Try them or experiment with your own recipes.

Master Recipe for Homemade Herb-Flavored Oil

Making herb-flavored oil is a great way to use up an abundance of herbs from a summer garden. Depending on the strength of the herbs you use, this oil should take anywhere from two to three weeks to make. Use flavored oils in pesto sauces, herb-flavored mayonnaise, salad dressing and with cold seafood and vegetables.

1 cup fresh herbs, left on the stems, if desired
1½ cups virgin or extra virgin olive oil

Thoroughly wash and dry the herbs and stuff into a 1½-cup mason jar or a clean bottle. Cover with the oil, seal tightly and let sit for two to three weeks in a cool, dark spot. After two weeks, taste the oil; it should have a definite herb flavor and aroma; if it is still weak, let it sit another few days. Strain the oil through a piece of cheesecloth and pour into a clean bottle or jar. Place a sprig or two of the fresh herbs into the jar before sealing. The oil can be refrigerated or left in a cool, dark spot. *Makes 1½ cups.*

Olive Oil Flavored with Garlic, Pepper and Bay Leaf

Use this oil with seafood and grilled meats. Brush on seafood, steaks or lamb shish kebab before broiling. Use in soups and stews and with salads.

> ½ cup olive oil, preferably extra virgin or virgin
> 2 whole cloves garlic, peeled
> 6 peppercorns
> 2 bay leaves

In a small, clean bottle or mason jar, place the garlic, peppercorns and bay leaves and cover with oil. (The oil should come up to the top of the jar.) Let sit 24 hours before using. *Makes ½ cup.*

Homemade Chinese Hot Chile Oil

This hot, spicy chile pepper oil is what gives Sichuan and Hunan dishes their fiery taste. There are many commercially produced chile oils on the market (see page 93), but many Chinese cooks feel they are too mild to be really effective.

Use this chile oil as you would a hot sauce—with soups, stews, egg dishes and Chinese noodles. Remember: this is lethal stuff—use it sparingly.

    1 cup peanut oil
    ¾ cup small dried red chile peppers, chopped
    2 to 3 teaspoons cayenne pepper
    1 teaspoon sesame oil (optional)

Heat the oil over a moderately high heat; do not let it boil or burn. Reduce the heat to low and add the chile peppers. Cover and let cook for about 10 minutes, or until the peppers turn black. Remove from the heat and let cool.

Once the oil is cool, stir in the cayenne pepper and sesame oil. Let the oil sit overnight and then strain through cheesecloth into a clean jar or bottle. Keep the oil refrigerated. *Makes 1 cup.*

Favorite Flavored-Oil Combinations

- Garlic, basil and crushed black peppercorn-flavored olive oil
- Olive oil with chopped fresh fennel and fennel seeds
- Peanut oil with ginger, garlic and shallots
- Sesame oil with chile peppers

- Fresh rosemary, thyme and oregano-flavored olive oil
- Olive oil with fresh coriander, Italian parsley and crushed coriander seeds
- Red and green chile pepper-flavored peanut oil
- Olive oil flavored with lemon wedges and cloves

COOKING WITH OIL

Broiled Fish Filets with Oil

This is a simple recipe for fish broiled with oil, lemon juice and pepper. You can use any type of oil you want with this recipe; nut oils—almond, hazelnut and walnut—are particularly good, but virgin olive, sesame and peanut oil are also delicious.

4 teaspoons oil (see note above)
1 pound of fish filets, such as sole, haddock or bluefish
   Generous grinding of black pepper
2 teaspoons lemon juice

Preheat the broiler. Spread 2 teaspoons of the oil on to the bottom of a shallow baking dish or an ovenproof skillet. Place the fish filets in the dish and sprinkle generously with pepper. Add the lemon juice and remaining 2 teaspoons of oil equally over the fish and broil for 5 to 7 minutes, or until the fish flakes easily when tested with a fork. Serve with lemon and lime wedges. *Serves 2.*

Sun-Dried Tomatoes Marinated in a Peppered Olive Oil

In Liguria, Italy, perfectly ripe plum tomatoes are dried out in the hot summer sun until they shrivel up and look like dried chile peppers. Like any other type of dried food, the tomatoes intensify in flavor; one sun-dried tomato tastes like a dozen fresh ones. They are sold in this country in two forms: dried, and marinated in a seasoned olive oil. Because the marinated tomatoes are so expensive, I prefer to buy the dried variety and marinate them myself.

It's definitely worth it to use a really good extra virgin olive oil with this marinade. Not only will the tomatoes soak up the olive flavor but, when the tomatoes are gone, you'll be left with a delicious tomato-pepper-flavored oil. Serve these tomatoes with fish, meats and chicken or in antipasto and salads. The flavored oil is wonderful over pasta salads and for sautéing fresh vegetables.

These tomatoes make a wonderful gift. Place the tomatoes in an attractive canning or mason jar, cover with the olive oil and seasonings, and seal the jar tightly. Place a label on the jar explaining how the tomatoes are used and give to a good friend.

> About 15 sun-dried tomatoes
> 1 small red chile pepper, crumbled
> 2 cloves garlic
> 2 bay leaves
> 4 black peppercorns
> 1 tablespoon pine nuts (optional)
> About ½ cup extra virgin olive oil

Place the tomatoes in a bowl and cover with lukewarm water. Let sit for about 15 minutes, or until soft. Drain and dry thoroughly on paper towels.

Into a small, clean mason jar (or old spice bottle), place half the chile pepper, 1 clove of garlic, 1 bay leaf, 2 peppercorns and ½ tablespoon of the nuts. Place half of the tomatoes on top and cover with about ¼ cup of oil. Place the remaining ingredients on top and cover with the remaining oil. (The oil should come to the top of the jar; add additional oil if needed.) Let sit for at least 24 hours before using.

Gingered Chicken Broth with Watercress, Scallions and Sesame Oil

This soothing chicken broth is spiked with the refreshing flavor of fresh ginger. A drop or two of hot sesame oil is added to each bowl of soup just before serving; it adds a wonderful nutty flavor without making the soup the least bit greasy or oily.

    4 cups chicken broth, preferably homemade
    4 thin slices fresh peeled ginger, about ¼ inch thick
    4 scallions, cut down the middle lengthwise and cut into
        2-inch pieces
    1 bunch watercress
    2 teaspoons Oriental sesame oil

In a medium-size saucepan, heat the chicken broth with the ginger over medium heat. Let simmer, covered, for about 5 minutes.

Add the scallions and watercress and let simmer until the greens are just soft, about 1 to 2 minutes. Meanwhile, heat the sesame oil in a small saucepan and let it get very hot, without burning or smoking. Add a few drops of the hot oil to each bowl of soup before serving. *Serves 4.*

Filet of Sole with Slivered Almonds
Sautéed in Almond Oil

2 tablespoons butter
2½ tablespoons almond oil
1 pound filet of sole
¼ cup flour, seasoned with salt and black pepper
½ cup slivered almonds
Lemon wedges

In a large skillet, melt the butter with 1 tablespoon of the oil over medium-high heat. Lightly flour the sole and when the butter and oil are hot, sauté the filets for about 2 minutes on each side. Transfer to a warm platter and cover to keep warm.

Add the remaining 1½ tablespoons of oil to the skillet and sauté the almonds until golden brown. Spoon the almonds over the sole and serve with lemon wedges. *Serves 2.*

Chinese-Style Scrambled Eggs with Sesame Oil

This recipe was inspired by my friend Ken Hom, a renowned Chinese chef and author of *Chinese Technique* (Simon & Schuster). Hom prepares eggs scrambled with sesame oil, bean sprouts and tiny Chinese eels in a wok. The sesame oil not only flavors them but also keeps them from sticking to the wok. This is a great brunch dish or just a new way to make an everyday breakfast a little bit different. I've omitted the eels.

    4 large eggs
1½ teaspoons Oriental sesame oil
  ¼ cup bean sprouts
  2 tablespoons thinly sliced scallions
  2 English muffins or pieces of toast

In a bowl, beat the eggs with 1 teaspoon of the sesame oil. Heat a wok or a skillet over high heat until it is very hot. Add the eggs and stir quickly; sprinkle in the sprouts and scallions and stir the eggs around until cooked, about 2 to 3 minutes. Serve on toasted English muffins or toast and drizzle with the remaining ½ teaspoon of sesame oil. *Serves 2.*

Sautéed Shrimp in
a Sesame Oil-Mustard-Orange-Soy Sauce

1½ tablespoons sesame oil
1 tablespoon virgin olive oil
3 cloves minced garlic
3 tablespoons minced fresh ginger
3 scallions, sliced down the center and cut into
    1½-inch pieces
1 pound small or medium shrimp, peeled
1 tablespoon Dijon or grainy mustard
½ cup fresh orange juice
1½ tablespoons light Chinese or Japanese soy sauce
    Freshly grated pepper to taste

In a wok or a large skillet, heat the oils over a high heat. Add the garlic and ginger and sauté for 2 to 3 seconds, or until lightly browned. Add the scallions and shrimp and sauté 1 minute. Whisk in the mustard, orange juice and soy sauce and let the sauce come to a boil; reduce the heat and let simmer about 4 to 5 minutes, or until the shrimp are cooked. Remove the shrimp with a slotted spoon to a warm serving platter and let the sauce boil for another minute, until slightly thickened. Pour over the shrimp and season with pepper to taste. Serve with rice or buttered noodles. *Serves 2 to 4.*

Coffee-Almond Slices

This buttery pound cake is flavored with almond oil and vanilla and baked in a bread tin that has been greased with almond oil. It is covered with a delicious, simple coffee-almond butter icing.

THE CAKE
2½ teaspoons almond oil
4 eggs, thoroughly beaten
¾ cup sugar
½ cup flour, sifted twice
¼ teaspoon vanilla

THE ICING
1 stick butter, softened
1 cup confectioners' sugar
About ¼ cup very strong coffee

THE GARNISH
1 tablespoon butter
1 teaspoon almond oil
½ cup slivered almonds

To make the pound cake: Preheat the oven to 350°. Lightly grease a bread tin with 1½ teaspoons of the almond oil and set aside. Place the eggs and sugar in a large bowl set over simmering water. Whisk vigorously until thickened, about 10 or 15 minutes. Remove from the heat and let the mixture cool slightly. Gently fold in the sifted flour and then mix in the remaining teaspoon of almond oil and the vanilla. Place the mixture into the greased tin and bake for 15 to 25 minutes, or until a toothpick inserted in the center comes out clean. Remove the cake from the pan and place on a cooling rack.

Meanwhile, *prepare the icing:* In a large bowl, cream the butter with the sugar until thoroughly blended and creamy. Mix in the coffee, a tablespoon at a time, until the icing turns a light coffee color and has a subtle coffee taste.

Prepare the garnish: In a small skillet, melt the butter and the almond oil over a moderately high heat. Sauté the almonds about 3 to 5 minutes, or until they turn a golden brown. Remove and drain on paper towels.

When the cake is cool, spread the top and sides with the icing and scatter the sautéed almonds along the top. Cut into thin slices and serve with strong coffee laced with Amaretto.

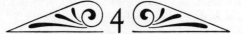

4

HOT PEPPER SAUCES AND HORSERADISHES

Salsas, Sambals, *Chinese Chile Sauces*, *Tabasco*, Wasabi

THERE ARE CERTAIN chapters in this book which will always be memorable for me. Olive oil, for example, turned out to be a luscious, sensual subject to write about. The tastings for that chapter were equally pleasant—exquisite extra virgin olive oils sprinkled over bowls of fresh pasta, thick slices of ripe tomatoes and chunks of crusty French bread. This chapter, on the other hand, was a bit different. It involved tears; it involved screaming and coughing; it involved fits of complete pain. After tasting close to one hundred different hot pepper sauces from around the world, I wondered if there was a clause in my insurance policy for severe indigestion.

Hot sauces are eaten around the world. In Japan a green horseradish root is ground into a fiery hot paste and eaten with *sushi* and *sashimi*; in Mexico, a mixture of chopped chile peppers, tomatoes, onions, spices and lime juice is used to season everything from corn tortillas to grilled steak. Red chile peppers ground with peanuts and tamarind juice are served with barbecued foods throughout Indonesia; and in Bermuda, chile peppers steeped in dry sherry are a favorite island tradition. In the United States, chile peppers, tomatoes, onions and spices are mixed to make a wide variety of sauces; and throughout China there are probably as many variations of chile sauce as there are chefs to create them.

Most hot pepper sauces are developed in countries with a tropical climate. For years I've heard that hot sauces will actually keep you cool when the weather is hot. And doctors and scientists have proven that chile peppers do stimulate the circulation and raise the temperature of your body. According to Jane Brody, health editor of *The New York Times,* "If you are living in a hot climate, the increase in body temperature can make you feel cooler by diminishing the difference between you and the surrounding air by inducing sweating, which cools the body when the perspiration evaporates."

Chile peppers are loaded with vitamins A and C and when they're ground up into a sauce, they can clear your sinuses, ease your asthma and stimulate your appetite. But the real appeal of a hot pepper sauce is its powerful flavor. A really good hot sauce takes you by the shoulders, gives you a good shake, and slaps your face to say "HELLO."

However, if you've eaten a hot sauce that just happens to be a bit too hot, don't reach for a glass of water, beer, wine or tea. Liquids scatter the oils in the chile pepper all over your tongue. What you want when the fire's too hot is to eat something that will soak up the peppery oils; try a piece of bread or a bite of noodles or rice. The most soothing thing possible after a bite of fire is to dip into a bowl of yogurt mixed with grated cucumber and chopped mint. It's like jumping into a swimming pool on a 100° day.

HOT SAUCE SURVEY

Chinese Chile Sauces

When I was about twelve years old, I remember my parents taking me to a restaurant in New York's Chinatown. To begin we had a plate of freshly made shrimp dumplings which arrived, much to my delight, with a choice of dipping sauces—hot Chinese mustard, a flavored soy sauce, gooey sweet duck sauce and a tiny bowl of bright-red Chinese chile sauce. I opted for the red stuff, submerged the dumpling into the tiny bowl and then, naively, popped the entire dumpling into my mouth. The next thing I remember was a stream of tears. But as the sauce crept down my throat, and I got my breath back, I suddenly realized this was an incredible taste sensation; I was hooked.

Chinese chile sauces can be overwhelming, but they can also be deliciously subtle. Each Chinese province is known for its own type of sauce, ranging from a simple blend of chile peppers, garlic and vinegar to more sophisticated black bean chile sauces. (See recipe on page 130.)

TASTING NOTES:
Chinese chile sauces tend to be thick. They are most often served as dipping sauces for grilled meats, roasted duck, chicken, spareribs, dumplings and savory pastries. Used sparingly, Chinese chile sauce can also add a wonderful peppery flavor to noodle and rice dishes and stir-fried foods.

BEST BRANDS:

Amofood Hot Sauce (Special)—This sauce says "HELLO." Made in Singapore, it's a very lethal combination of chiles, soybeans, oil, sugar, salt and spices. Once it goes down your throat it spreads around and then slowly attacks. It is definitely for machos only.

B. B. Pure Hot Sauce—This is a superb hot sauce—"a pyromaniac's delight," as one friend of mine describes it. It's made in Taiwan from fresh red chile peppers, soybeans, vinegar and spices. Try it on french fries.

Garlic Pepper Sauce—The Southeast Asia Company of Baldwin Park, California, imports this wonderful condiment. It is a thick, bright-red sauce full of garlic and ground red chile peppers. Grill it on oysters and clams, shrimp or scallops, or use as a dipping sauce for barbecued chicken and meat. It's also fantastic in a cold Chinese noodle dish with sesame sauce.

Koon Yuck Wah Kee Chilli Sauce—Made in Hong Kong, this is a particularly unique sauce due to the addition of sweet potatoes. It has a terrific thick, creamy texture and a very hot, spicy flavor. Broil it on scallops or use as a spicy dip for raw vegetables or fried chicken.

Lingham's Chilly Sauce—This is a thick, slightly sweet sauce that goes well with all sorts of Chinese and Oriental foods. Made by Lingham and Son of Malaysia, it is mildly spicy.

May Lin China Black Bean Hot Sauce—I think this is an outrageously good sauce. Made from Chinese black beans, chile peppers, garlic, mustard and soy sauce, it is intensely hot. It makes a great dipping sauce for dumplings, shrimp and steamed clams. Serve it with grilled steak, pan-fried fish filets and stir-fried vegetables.

Roland Hot Chili Sauce (Oriental-Style)—Made in Taiwan, this dark-red sauce is a bit thinner than most of the other Chinese chile sauces but just as hot. It's great on noodles and with spring rolls.

Satan Brand Hot Sauce—Yes, I do believe the Devil has something to do with this sauce. Made in the Philippines, its bright reddish-orange color is a definite warning of what's to come.

Yeo's Hot Chili Sauce—"This is an exotic piquant sauce of the highest quality, specially blended in the Orient to impart a spicy, appetizing taste to both Asian and European cuisine," says the label on this hot and slightly sour sauce. Made in Singapore, it's delicious with oysters, clams and shrimp, or grilled on chicken and butterflied lamb. Yeo's also makes an excellent *Sweet Chili Sauce*. Made from chiles, tamarind, sugar, lime and spices, it's terrific with dumplings, noodle dishes and over a sliced avocado, tomato and onion salad.

Harissa (*Moroccan Hot Sauces*)

Harissa, made from a blend of dried red chile peppers, salt, lemon juice and spices, is a fiery-hot Tunisian sauce. It's traditionally served with *couscous*, a fine grain (made from semolina flour) which is steamed and served with a spicy stew (usually made of lamb or chicken with large chunks of fresh vegetables). The *couscous* is served in a large bowl and the meat and vegetable stew and its broth are ladled on top. A small dab of *harissa* is mixed into the broth to give the dish an extra peppery bolt.

TASTING NOTES:

In addition to *couscous*, *harissa* also adds delicious flavor to soups, stews, pasta sauces, goulash, rice dishes, cold meats and grilled fish. Many of the commercially made brands of *harissa* sold in the United States are super thick and pasty; you may want to thin them out with fresh lemon juice and olive oil. Although some of these brands of *harissa* have a good, hot bite, nothing can compare with a freshly made *harissa*; see page 131 for the recipe.

BEST BRANDS:

Harissa Dea—Made in France, this is a very spicy brand of *harissa*. It's superb with lamb *couscous* and beef curry.

Harissa de la Mauresque—Peppers, oil, garlic, coriander, cumin and lemon juice make this French-made *harissa* distinctive. It should be used in very small quantities.

Horseradish

When I was a kid, horseradish was always a staple item in our refrigerator. We ate it on brisket and potato pancakes, gefilte fish and dark rye bread, roast beef and thin slices of boiled ham. But for years, I never realized that horseradish came from a root; to me it was always just that hot white stuff in a jar.

A relative of the mustard family, horseradish is the most pungent of all edible roots. It is native to Eastern Europe and Western Asia; it grows wild and is also cultivated throughout Europe, England and the United States.

No one seems to know how horseradish got its name. But Steven Gold, whose family has been making horseradish in Brooklyn, New York, since 1932, offers one possible explanation. According to Gold, horseradish comes from the German word *"Meerrettich,"* meaning "sea radish." Horseradish, he claims, grew wild along the seashore and was also sometimes known as "the galloping radish," which may have led to its name.

For hundreds of years, horseradish was prized as a medicinal herb. In the first century, Pliny claimed horseradish would dissolve gallstones and help cure asthma. And there are still some people who swear by it for clearing sinuses and curing a winter cold. Like hot chile peppers, fresh horseradish is loaded with vitamin C.

It wasn't until the sixteenth century that horseradish was used for culinary purposes. In *Stalking the Healthful Herbs*, Euell Gibbons writes: "One herbalist finally mentions its use by the Germans 'as a sauce to eat fish with and such meats as we do mustarde,' but it is not until 1640 that a writer mentions its use as a condiment in England, and he damns it with faint praise, writing that it is used only by 'country people and strong laboring men,' and adding 'it is too strong for tender and gentle stomachs.' Not long after, however, horseradish did begin to appear on the tables of the gentry."

Today the biting, pungent flavor of horseradish is one of the most popular condiments in England. Roast beef served with freshly grated horseradish sauce has become as commonplace as a hamburger with ketchup. In the United States, horseradish has become increasingly popular in the last few years. You now find it in fancy restaurants served with raw fish, smoked fish and meats. Horseradish is used in a wide variety of sauces and is frequently found floating in glasses of spicy Bloody Marys.

TASTING NOTES:
- Serve horseradish with roast beef, smoked ham, tongue or lamb.
- A pot of horseradish should always be on the table when serving corned beef and cabbage or a boiled beef dinner.
- Horseradish goes particularly well with fish—raw oysters and clams on the half shell, smoked fish (particularly trout), boiled shrimp and crabs.
- Around the Jewish holidays horseradish can be found more easily in many grocery stores. Horseradish is one of the five symbolic foods traditionally placed on the Seder plate at Passover; it symbolizes the suffering the Jews felt when they fled Egypt. Horseradish is also served with other Jewish foods—gefilte fish, boiled beef, brisket and herring.

- In France, fresh horseradish root is brought to the table and each person slices off a small piece and sprinkles it generously with coarse sea salt. It is said to stimulate the appetite.
- Horseradish mixed with grated apple and sour cream is delicious with *schnitzel*, pork chops, or thin slices of roast ham.
- Add horseradish to a Bloody Mary; it gives the drink a spicy punch and nice texture.
- Mix freshly grated horseradish into a cocktail sauce and serve with boiled shrimp, raw clams or fried oysters.
- Shave thin slices off a fresh horseradish root and serve on top of a grilled steak.
- Add a teaspoon of horseradish to a spicy Dijon mustard and spread it on top of fish filets and broil. It makes a spicy horseradish-mustard glaze.
- Mix horseradish into a homemade mayonnaise (see page 161 for the recipe) and use as the base for a turkey, egg or chicken salad.
- Try serving boiled new potatoes or steamed asparagus with a simple sauce made of melted butter, a few teaspoons of prepared horseradish and chopped fresh dill.
- Other ideas for using horseradish are on pages 140–44.

BEST BRANDS:

Horseradish does not keep for a long time. After about two to four months, it loses its "zip." Buy only a small amount at a time, or better yet, make your own; see recipe on page 138.

Gold's Real Home Style Horseradish—In 1932, Tillie Gold began making horseradish in the Gold family's small Coney Island, New York, apartment. Today Gold's claims to be *the* best-selling brand of horseradish. (The Gold's root cellar, located on McDonald Avenue in Brooklyn, is the largest in the world—a full city block long, stacked 10 feet high with fresh horseradish root from around the world.) During the Jewish holidays, the Gold's horseradish factory produces 1.5 million bottles of horseradish *a day*. It's been made using the original family recipe for over fifty years. They make a *Regular White Horseradish*, a *Creamy Hot Style* (watch out) and a *Red Horseradish* with fresh beets. Gold's horseradish is the best.

Helluva Good Horseradish—"One taste is worth a thousand words," says the label. This fresh-tasting horseradish is made in Sodus, New York. It's fantastic on thinly sliced buttered black bread with roast beef.

Tulkoff's Horseradish—Made in Maryland, this is impressive stuff. Sol Tulkoff, president of Tulkoff's Horseradish, takes horseradish very seriously. In his factory, east of Baltimore's inner harbor, Tulkoff has established a special horseradish museum with over fifty paintings of horseradish roots. Tulkoff's makes four varieties of freshly grated horseradish—*Regular White* or *Red* and *"Extra Hot" White* or *"Extra Hot" Red.*

Indian Hot Sauces

In India they are called hot oil pickles, but to me they seem more like thick, chunky sauces. Ultimately, it's a matter of semantics. What counts with these condiments is their intense heat. They're made from all sorts of fruits and spices—mangoes, limes, lemons, eggplants, ginger and lotus stem—but the crucial ingredient is the chile pepper. These Indian pickles are, above all else, tremendously hot. To place them anywhere else in this book would be inappropriate.

Indian pickles are quite different in taste and texture from Western pickles. The fruits are preserved in oil with a variety of spices and chile peppers and they eventually "dissolve" into a thick, fiery-hot sauce. Indian pickles must be eaten in minute quantities and always with other foods.

TASTING NOTES:
Indian pickles are traditionally eaten with curries, particularly vegetable and seafood curries. They also go well with grilled chicken, barbecued meats, and Indian breads and deep-fried savory pastries.

[115]

BEST BRANDS:

Patak's Brinjal Pickle (Eggplant)—This pickle has a wonderful, rich eggplant flavor. It's slightly sweet and full of spicy chile peppers. Serve it with chicken or vegetable curries, dumplings or savory pastries.

Patak's Extra Hot Mango Pickle—I don't care how macho you may think you are, this one is spicy. It's also slightly sweet and gives grilled meats and barbecued chicken an authentic Indian flavor. Made from mangoes, mustard, chile peppers, oil and spices, it's wonderful with curries, roasted chicken or mixed with yogurt as a dip. It's also great on crackers with cream cheese. Be careful, this pickle can be dangerous.

Priya Sweet Ginger Pickle in Oil with Garlic—Made from ginger, tamarind, sesame oil, garlic, chile powder, jaggery (unrefined palm sugar) and spices, this is a thick, almost pasty sauce. The word "sweet" on the label is a total misnomer; this sauce is, above all else, spicy and terribly hot. The combination of ginger and chile peppers is, however, a delicious one. Use with Chinese stir-fries, shrimp curry, broiled fish, and vegetable stews.

Sanjus Hot South India Green Chilli Pickle in Oil—This sauce is guaranteed to kill your enemies and any unwanted relatives. It's pure, outrageous, unbearable fire. This is a thick green sauce made from green chile peppers, sesame oil, mustard, fenugreek (a spice), garlic, oil and vinegar. Produced in southern India, this chile pickle should be used at your own risk.

Sanjus South Indian Lime Pickle in Oil—Distinctively tart and spicy, this mixture includes limes, sesame oil, red chile peppers, mustard and fenugreek. Serve with seafood curries, broiled fish or chicken.

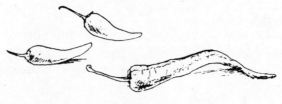

Mexican Salsas *and* Other Latin American Hot Pepper Sauces

There are over one hundred varieties of chile peppers growing throughout Latin America, so it's no wonder that they are such an important part of the diet. There is an equally astounding number of *salsas* (sauces) made from these peppers. They can be raw or cooked and range from mildly spicy to "oh-my-God-please-help-me" hot.

The most familiar is the Mexican *salsa picante* (hot sauce) or *salsa cruda* (raw sauce)—both are combinations of chopped fresh tomatoes, onions, chile peppers (usually serrano or jalapeño), lime juice (or vinegar), salt and spices. *Salsa picante* is the basis for a number of other hot sauces. The Chilean pepper sauce called *pebre* uses the same ingredients, with the addition of olive oil. Throughout Texas and New Mexico, there are now hundreds of *salsa picantes*, each with its own slight variation.

Salsa verde (green sauce) is another popular hot sauce made from *tomatillos*, Mexican green husk tomatoes. *Tomatillos* have a distinctive flavor, quite different from regular green tomatoes, and when they are chopped and mixed with fresh *cilantro* (coriander), chile peppers, onions and garlic, they make a spicy and somewhat sour sauce.

Salsa ranchera (country sauce) is a simple combination of tomatoes, chile peppers, garlic and onions cooked in oil. It is the classic accompaniment to *huevos rancheros*—a Mexican breakfast dish of fried eggs served on freshly made tortillas.

TASTING NOTES:

Mexican *salsas* and Latin American pepper sauces go best with simply cooked foods—fried eggs, grilled steak, barbecued chicken, pork and pan-fried fish. Of course, they also go well with more traditional Mexican food—tacos, tortillas, guacamole and taco chips, *burritos*, enchiladas, *quesadillas* and *tostadas*.

[117]

The traditional way to enjoy these sauces is to make up a small batch at home. Although there are now hundreds of terrific *salsas* sold in ethnic and specialty food stores across the country, the bottled sauces never seem to match the flavor and texture of a freshly made hot pepper sauce. (See recipes on pages 133–35.) Listed below are a few of my favorite sauces.

BEST BRANDS:

Casa Peña Blanca Chili Chilpotle Sauce—Casa Peña Blanca is the name of a small, family-owned company in El Paso, Texas. They make a number of wonderful Mexican and Southwestern condiments, all based on old family recipes. This musty, smokey-flavored chile sauce is one of their best. It's a thick, spicy sauce made from a blend of smokey chile chilpotle peppers. It's fantastic served with eggs scrambled with bits of avocado, tomato and onion. It also makes a great dip mixed with sour cream and served with raw vegetables, tacos and *nachos.*

Casa Peña Blanca Tomatillo Sauce—I absolutely adore this sauce. It brings back vivid memories of the tastes and smells of Mexico. Made from *tomatillos* (Mexican green husk tomatoes), chile peppers, onions, garlic, oil, vinegar and spices, it is a thin, very spicy sauce. Serve with tortillas and tacos, or over fried eggs, grilled steak and hamburgers. It also makes a great dipping sauce for crab, shrimp, barbecued chicken, and tacos and guacamole.

Desert Rose Homemade Salsas—Created in the Tucson, Arizona, kitchen of Patti and Steve Swidler, there are two types of Desert Rose *salsas.* The *Medium Salsa* has a fresh tomato flavor and a subtle degree of heat. The *Hot Salsa* is . . . *hot.* These sauces look like pasta sauces; they're thick and tomatoey and delicious added to soups, stews, chile, dips and fried eggs. As the brochure says, "When the chips are down, make sure they're in Desert Rose."

Hell On The Red—Two devils use their pitchforks to point to a map of Telephone, Texas, the home of this very hot sauce. Made from tomatoes, onions, lots of jalapeño peppers, garlic and spices, it makes a great dipping sauce for taco chips.

Herdez Salsa Verde—This Mexican green chile sauce is powerful

[118]

and should be used with caution. Herdez also makes a delicious *Salsa Casera* (red chile sauce) and a *Salsa Ranchera*.

La Victoria Salsa Picante—This Mexican sauce is readily available in most large grocery stores across the country and it's surprisingly good. La Victoria also makes a *Salsa Ranchera* and *Salsa Victoria*. The degree of heat is indicated by a thermometer printed on the label.

Old San Antonio Salsa Mexicana—The Old San Antonio Company of San Antonio, Texas, makes excellent hot sauces. Their *Salsa Mexicana* is a particular favorite. Made from tomatoes, jalapeño peppers, onions, vinegar and spices, it is exceedingly hot. They also make superb *Salsa Ranchera*.

Pecos River Hot Green Taco Sauce—Jane Butel, author of *The Tex-Mex Cookbook* and *Chili Madness*, created this very fresh-tasting, spicy sauce. Made in New Mexico, it goes well with all sorts of Mexican, Tex-Mex and New Mexican cuisine.

Santa Cruz Hot Taco Sauce—This delicious sauce comes from Tumacacori, Arizona. It's made from chile peppers, sesame oil, garlic, onions, tomatoes and spices. Santa Cruz also makes an excellent *Mild Taco Sauce* and *Green Salsa*. Serve any of these sauces as a dip for tacos and guacamole or with barbecued chicken or meat.

Tampico Salsa Picante—This is the Mexican version of Tabasco sauce. It has a wonderful peppery, vinegary flavor that goes well with all sorts of foods.

Sambals

Sambals are fiery-hot pepper sauces that are served with a wide variety of Southeast Asian dishes. The word *"sambal"* describes a range of condiments—from an exotic mixture of chile peppers blended with garlic, shallots, tamarind juice and shrimp paste to a peanut-butter-based sauce. A *sambal* can be raw or cooked, killer-hot or mild, but the one thing all *sambals* have in common is hot chile peppers.

Sambals are most commonly eaten with Indonesian food. They are an important part of the traditional Indonesian banquet called *rijsttafel* ("rice table"). The banquet consists of a huge plate of boiled rice, surrounded by some twenty to thirty "side" dishes, of which at least four or five are *sambals*. Critics often judge *rijsttafel* according to the number and quality of homemade *sambals* served.

Indonesians take their *sambals* seriously. An old Indonesian proverb declares that even an "ugly girl" can find a husband if she can brew good coffee and make a good *sambal*.

TASTING NOTES:
There are as many uses for *sambals* as there are types. They complement mild-flavored rice dishes, grilled beef, pork or chicken *satay*, egg rolls, noodle dishes, broiled shrimp and stir-fried vegetables. Serve *sambals* as you would a hot pepper sauce or spicy relish.

BEST BRANDS:
Conimex is a Dutch company that makes a wide variety of Indonesian condiments and foods. They make four excellent *sambals*: *Sambal Asem* is a thick, spicy blend of tamarind, onions and spices that goes particularly well with broiled fish, rice dishes and curries. *Sambal Badjak* is a piquant sauce that tastes like home-fried onions and peppers. Made from red chile peppers, onions, peanut oil, spices and candlenuts, it is terrific with lamb curries, vegetable stew and grilled steak. *Sambal Manis* is a milder *sambal* made from fried

hot chile peppers, onions and spices. It's especially good with noodle dishes, spring rolls and curries. *Sambal Oelek,* a spicy mixture of ground red chile peppers, salt and spices, has a thick, ketchup-like consistency. It's excellent in pasta sauces, curries and on top of fried eggs.

Go Tan Sambals—This Dutch company makes three excellent varieties of *sambal. Sambal Ojeroek* is a pungent combination of fried red peppers with citrus; *Sambal Badjak* (fried red peppers and onions) is fantastic on steak and with stir-fried vegetables; *Sambal Oelek* (crushed red peppers and salt) is excellent with eggs, burgers and curries.

May Lin China Inc.'s Sambal Oeleck—Based on a Vietnamese recipe, this bright-red peppery mixture will make your lips tingle. It's very hot, very spicy and very good. Try it on steaks, noodles and in sauces.

Noy Fong Foods Sambal Oelek—This *sambal* adds a great, spicy flavor to Thai noodle dishes and chicken or pork *satay.*

Southeast Asia Food Co.'s Sambal Oelek—Watch out. A little bit of this *sambal* goes a long way. Use it as you would any hot pepper sauce, only do so with extreme caution.

Sherry Peppers Sauce

Bermuda has long been famous for its beautiful sandy beaches, idyllic scenery, and vacationing honeymooners. But one of the island's few native products has recently gained an international reputation.

Sherry peppers sauce is made by steeping hot chile peppers and spices in casks of dry sherry. After several months, the liquid is transformed into a spicy, hot pepper sauce. Yeaton Outerbridge, a native Bermudian, has been bottling sherry peppers sauce since 1964, but the history of the sauce goes back many years. According

[121]

to Outerbridge: "Bermudians first came to know sherry peppers back in the sailing vessel days of the Royal Navy. After several months at sea, the quality of the food aboard ship attained a degree of ripeness that made a strongly flavored seasoning a necessity. An enterprising officer ashore in Bermuda saw the small native 'bird' pepper. This was a particularly 'hot' pepper which the officer thought might be used to disguise the taste of the provisions aboard and make them palatable. So he took the peppers, steeped them in sherry and . . . a new condiment was born."

TASTING NOTES:
Sherry peppers sauce can be used like a regular hot pepper sauce, but the sherry gives it a very unique flavor. It's particularly good in soups and fish chowders, in sauces, marinades and barbecue sauce. Sprinkle it over fried eggs, fried tomatoes and pan-fried fish. (See page 137 for a recipe for making your own homemade version of sherry peppers sauce.)

BEST BRAND:
Outerbridge's Original Sherry Peppers Sauce—This is the most popular type of sherry peppers sauce sold in Bermuda. Made from peppers and selected spices steeped in dry sherry for several months, it's truly delicious. Use sparingly; it's hot.

Tabasco Sauce and Other Louisiana Hot Sauces

After tasting over a hundred different hot pepper sauces from around the world, I've come to the inevitable conclusion that Tabasco is the best. It has a perfect balance of heat and good peppery flavor—a punch, but not a knockout.

The history of Tabasco is one of those great American success stories. It begins with the McIlhenny family; the place is Avery Island, Louisiana, a narrow, 2,500-acre stretch of land jutting above the Gulf Coast. Avery Island is not really an "island"; it's actually an oversized hill built on top of a large salt dome. The Avery and McIlhenny families have owned the "island" since 1818 and for years the main industry there was salt mining. But in 1848 all that changed.

A friend of Edmund McIlhenny, named "Gleason," returned from the Mexican War bringing with him hot Mexican chile peppers. Gleason raved about the peppers' spicy taste and their ability to enhance the flavors of other foods. McIlhenny decided to sow the pepper seeds at his father-in-law's plantation on Avery Island, and before long he had a field of bright-red peppers.

Then McIlhenny had an idea. He wanted to capture the spicy essence of these exotic peppers in a sauce. After many failed experiments, he developed what he called the "perfect hot pepper sauce." In 1868, McIlhenny filled 350 bottles with the bright-red spicy liquid and sold them to select wholesalers across the country. It was a hit. By 1870, he had received orders for over a thousand bottles. Just two years later the demand for the sauce had grown so great that McIlhenny opened a branch in London in order to accommodate the orders that were pouring in from Great Britain and Europe. Today the McIlhenny family produces 200,000 to 300,000 bottles of Tabasco sauce *a day*. Their sauce has become so famous around the world that the name "Tabasco" has practically become a generic term for all hot pepper sauces.

The recipe for Tabasco sauce hasn't changed much over the years. It all starts with tabasco peppers, a strain of peppers developed by McIlhenny. (The word *"tabasco"* is an Indian term meaning "where the soil is humid." And it is the heat and moisture of the Southern soil that helps the tabasco pepper develop its distinctive flavor.)

Tabasco sauce is made by a slow, precise process. In early spring the tabasco pepper seedlings are transplanted from greenhouses and hotbeds to the fields of Avery Island. In the next few months, the land is transformed into a kind of magical carpet; peppers in different stages of growth—oranges, yellows and reds—pop up from the rich earth in a wild splash of color.

In the late summer, the ripe red peppers are harvested. They are crushed with Avery Island rock salt to create a "mash," and then placed into white oak barrels covered with perforated lids. A layer of rock salt is spread over the top of the lid to keep air out and let gases escape. The mash is allowed to ferment and develop flavor for close to three years. It is then inspected (often by Walter McIlhenny, president of the McIlhenny Co. and grandson of its founder) for color, aroma and flavor. The mash that passes inspection is then blended with distilled vinegar and placed into 2,000-gallon oak vats. For four weeks, the mixture is gently stirred with wooden paddles. The sauce is then strained and filtered before being placed into the traditional, thin-necked Tabasco bottle.

TASTING NOTES:
I use Tabasco with just about everything. The little red bottle sits on the table through every meal; I just can't get enough of it.

Tabasco can be used as a table condiment or you can cook with it. You should always remember that, like garlic and onions, the longer it cooks the more its flavor dissipates. The best way to taste the flavor of Tabasco is to add it just before serving so it has a chance to heat through and not disappear.

Here are a few of my favorite ways to use Tabasco:

- Try sprinkling a few drops on fried, scrambled or poached eggs. It's also terrific in a red-and-green-pepper omelette.
- Add Tabasco to raw clams and oysters on the half shell.
- Sprinkle a few drops into soups, stews and casseroles just before serving.
- Serve with sautéed fish, fried clams and cold boiled shrimp.
- Try adding a few drops to a Bloody Mary to give it a spicy bite.
- Sprinkle a few drops of Tabasco on steaks, chicken and shish kebab just a few minutes before they're done being broiled or grilled.
- Add Tabasco to pasta sauces just before you toss it with the pasta.
- Add to marinades and sauces instead of black pepper or peppercorns.

[124]

- I have a friend who swears Tabasco adds an amazing flavor to apple and pumpkin pies; try it.
- Sprinkle Tabasco, instead of ketchup, on french fries and hamburgers.
- Add a few drops of Tabasco sauce to a homemade (or even a bottled) barbecue sauce to give it an extra bite.

Other Louisiana Hot Pepper Sauces

Tabasco may be the king, but there are a number of other excellent Louisiana-made hot pepper sauces. Listed here are just a few.

BEST BRANDS:
Evangeline Tabasco Peppers—Tiny green tabasco peppers steeped in vinegar are all there is to this hot, pungent sauce. You can shake the peppery vinegar onto salads, steaks, grilled chops or broiled tomatoes. Sprinkle into soups and gumbos or use to make a dipping sauce. When you're through with the sauce, you're left with deliciously hot pickled peppers. Made in St. Martinville, Louisiana, this is a wonderful sauce.

Horseshoe Brand Louisiana Red Hot Sauce—This New Orleans-made sauce, chock-full of ground cayenne peppers, is excellent on fish and shellfish. It's a bit salty but has a good spicy flavor.

Texarkana Hellfire Sauce—"Hellfire" may be pushing it, but this is definitely hot stuff. Made in St. Martinville, Louisiana, for Texarkana, a trendy restaurant located on West 10th Street in Manhattan, this is a thick peppery blend nicely spiked with ground cumin. Serve it with grilled meats, in sauces, soups and gumbos or as a dip with taco chips. Texarkana also makes a delicious *Louisiana Green Hot Sauce.* Made from young cayenne peppers that are aged in brine for a year, the sauce is hot and slightly sweet.

Trappey's Red Devil Louisiana Hot Sauce—The label on this sauce tells the story of what's inside: The Devil takes his pitchfork and punctures the juice out of a patch of red-hot chile peppers. That spicy essence, mixed with vinegar and salt, makes one hell of a good sauce. Use on eggs, meats, fish or in soups, sauces and salads.

Thai Hot Chile Sauce (Nam Prik)

Some time ago, while I was sitting at Bangkok Cuisine, my favorite Thai restaurant in Boston, I overheard the following conversation: "Well, what do you think? Isn't Thai food fantastic?" a young male student asked his female companion. "It's okay," she replied, "but the condiments are outrageous." She was referring to the platter of pungent Thai fish sauce, chopped peanuts, pickled chile peppers, flakes of dried red chile peppers, and fiery-hot pepper sauce that is served with every meal.

Thai hot sauce, or *Nam Prik*, is found on tables throughout Thailand. According to Jennifer Brennan, author of *The Original Thai Cookbook*, "*Nam Prik* sauce is the universal favorite of the Thai people through all strata of society. It is one of the ancient, traditional dishes of the country, records indicating that it was probably eaten in the twelfth and thirteenth centuries during the Sukhothai period. . . ."

Brennan goes on to say that "every meal will be accompanied by at least one or two sauces and they play as important a part within their cuisine as the French sauces do within their cuisine." Essentially, *Nam Prik* is made from ground chiles, vinegar, salt and sugar. Other common ingredients include peanuts, garlic, shallots, coconut cream, fish sauce, dried shrimp, shrimp paste, raw eggplant, and tamarind liquid. *Nam Prik* is generally thick and gooey like ketchup. (See recipe for making your own on page 129.)

Saus Prik is a sweeter version of *Nam Prik*. Made with the addition of sugar, raisins, tomatoes and sweet jam, it's particularly popular with seafood and spring rolls.

TASTING NOTES:
Thai hot sauces go well with all sorts of Oriental cuisine—curries, light soups, rice dishes, grilled meats and noodles. *Pad Thai*, a Thai fried noodle dish with shrimp, bean sprouts, fresh coriander and ground peanuts is superb topped with a teaspoon of Thai hot

sauce. These sauces are also good mixed in a chicken or cold beef salad, or served with fried chicken, barbecued pork or spareribs and with fried or scrambled eggs.

BEST BRANDS:
Chili Sauce—Made in Bangkok (and imported by Eastimpex of San Francisco), this sauce has a label that is written completely in Thai. Made from chile peppers, vinegar, garlic, salt and sugar, this is a delicious but deceptive sauce. It tastes fairly mild at first but then the fire creeps, slowly, down your throat; watch out.
Siracha Chile Sauce—Originally made and sold locally in the seaside town of Siracha, this hot sauce can now be found in Thai and Oriental food stores across the United States. There are three varieties available—mild, medium and hot.
Sweet Chilli Sauce (Tuố'ng Cȟâm Khô Múc)—Made in Bangkok, this is a particularly thick, spicy sauce. It's a bit sweet and goes well with stir-fried vegetables, chicken and curries.

Wasabi (*Japanese Green Horseradish*)

Wasabi, the Japanese word for "mountain hollyhock," is a green horseradish root that grows wild throughout Japan on flooded mountain terraces and at the edge of cold, clear streams. Fresh *wasabi* root cannot be cultivated and is almost impossible to buy in this country. However, dry powdered *wasabi* can be found in Oriental markets and specialty food stores.

Wasabi is more fragrant and sharp than white horseradish. A teaspoon of ground *wasabi* has a potent, powerful bite that will clear your sinuses within seconds. Like other hot, peppery foods, *wasabi* stimulates the appetite and is rich in vitamin C.

[127]

TASTING NOTES:

Wasabi is sold in powdered or paste form. The powdered *wasabi* is preferable because it never goes bad and you can mix it up as you need it.

Similar to powdered mustard; simply add a small amount of tepid water to the *wasabi* powder and mix until it forms a smooth, thick paste. Let the paste stand for about 10 minutes to develop full flavor.

The most popular use for *wasabi* is mixed into soy sauce to make a dipping sauce for *sushi* and *sashimi*. In addition, *wasabi* is dabbed on-to the rice in *sushi* rolls to give the raw fish a fresh, cleansing flavor. (It is also believed that *wasabi* disguises any unpleasant flavors of the raw fish.)

Wasabi is also delicious served with grilled meats and chicken. A touch of *wasabi* mixed with Japanese rice vinegar and a light peanut oil makes a delicious salad dressing for mixed greens or steamed vegetables. Try spreading a small dab of *wasabi* on shrimp, fish filets or raw oysters before broiling.

BEST BRANDS:

The following brands of *wasabi*, all produced in Japan, are excellent.

House Neri Wasabi (Prepared Japanese Horseradish)—Packaged in a small tube, this is a delicious, spicy combination of powdered *wasabi*, vegetable oil and salt.

Kaneku Brand Wasabi—This powdered *wasabi* root comes in small one-ounce tins.

Kin-Jirushi—This is a pungent, powdered *wasabi*.

Wasabi-Ko Powdered Horseradish—This is my favorite brand of *wasabi*. It comes in small one-ounce tins decorated with an illustration of the potent green root.

MAKING YOUR OWN HOT SAUCES

If you have friends who love hot, peppery foods, these hot sauces make ideal gifts. Simply place the sauce in a clean jar or bottle and write out a label describing the contents of the sauce, with a warning of just how hot it really is.

Nam Prik (*Thai Hot Sauce*)

This recipe comes from Jennifer Brennan's *The Original Thai Cookbook* (Richard Marek Publishers, 1981). Serve it with fish, noodle dishes, chicken and grilled meat. The sauce keeps well for several weeks, refrigerated, and even tastes better after a day or so.

2 tablespoons whole, dried shrimp, chopped
6 cloves garlic, chopped
4 dried red chile peppers (including seeds), chopped
1 teaspoon granulated sugar
3 tablespoons fish sauce (*nam pla*) (see page 171)
3 tablespoons lime juice
2 fresh red or green serrano chiles, seeded and finely chopped

In a mortar or food processor, pound or grind the shrimp, garlic, dried chiles and sugar until the mixture is well blended. Gradually add the fish sauce and lime juice, a spoonful at a time, until you have a smooth mixture. Pour in a serving bowl and stir in the fresh chiles. *Makes about ½ cup.*

Chinese Chile and Black Bean Sauce

Chile peppers, black beans, sesame oil, garlic, ginger and Sichuan peppercorns all go into making this thick, spicy sauce. Serve it with dumplings, stir-fried vegetables, seafood and Chinese noodle dishes.

¼ cup chile powder
2 cloves garlic
1 tablespoon Chinese black beans, rinsed and finely chopped
2½ tablespoons sesame oil
2 tablespoons peanut oil
1½ teaspoons chopped fresh ginger
5 Sichuan or black peppercorns
1 small dried red chile pepper, chopped with seeds
1 scallion, chopped

In a small serving bowl, mix the chile powder, garlic and black beans and reserve.

In a small skillet, heat the sesame and peanut oil over a high heat. Add the ginger, peppercorns, chile pepper and scallion and cook for about 3 to 4 minutes, or until the ginger and scallion begin to turn golden brown. Remove the skillet from the heat and let cool a few minutes.

Strain the flavored oil over the chile mixture, discarding the ginger, peppercorns, chile and scallion, and stir to form a smooth, thick sauce. Let the sauce sit for about 30 minutes before serving, or place in a clean, clear jar and cover and store in a cool spot for up to four months. *Makes about ½ cup.*

Harissa

The fire-engine-red color of *harissa* is a sign of what's to come; when freshly made, *harissa* is hotter than hot. (You'll be screaming for the fire extinguisher.) But once it's given a chance to sit for a while, the flavors of the lemon juice and cumin mixed with the chile create a wonderfully unique condiment.

Used sparingly, *harissa* adds zest to *couscous*, stews, soups and casseroles; it's also great served with thin slices of cold lamb or beef. Mix a bit into a homemade mayonnaise to make a spicy dip for cold shrimp and raw vegetables.

    1 cup dried red chile peppers
    2 teaspoons salt
    2 cloves garlic
       About 2 tablespoons lemon juice
    1 teaspoon ground cumin powder
       Olive oil

Place the chiles in a medium saucepan and cover with cold water. Place over a high heat and let the water come to a boil. Remove from the heat and let sit for about an hour.

Drain the chiles and place in a blender or food processor along with the salt and garlic. Blend the mixture and add the lemon juice, bit by bit, to keep the mixture moving. (If the peppers don't seem to be blending, add additional lemon juice as needed.) Once the mixture is thoroughly blended, remove and place in a small glass jar. Stir in the cumin and smooth the mixture down. Pour enough olive oil over the *harissa* to completely cover the top. Cover and refrigerate. *Makes about ½ cup.*

Moroccan Hot Sauce

This is an adaptation of a traditional Moroccan hot pepper sauce called Sauce Chermella. If you like the musty, exotic flavor of cumin, then you'll love this peppery mixture. It goes well with all sorts of barbecued foods, with *couscous*, as a marinade for chicken, shrimp, swordfish or lamb, and as a dipping sauce for raw vegetables and avocados. One of the best ways to eat this hot sauce is in a toasted pita bread sandwich filled with thinly sliced barbecued lamb.

½ teaspoon cayenne pepper
1 teaspoon peanut oil
2 cloves garlic, chopped
1 small fresh chile pepper, stemmed and with seeds
1½ tablespoons fresh, chopped coriander
1 tablespoon cumin powder
1½ teaspoons paprika
1 teaspoon salt
2 tablespoons red wine vinegar
1½ tablespoons water
2½ tablespoons olive oil

In a small bowl, mix the cayenne pepper and the oil and let sit at room temperature for 30 minutes.

Place all the remaining ingredients except the olive oil into a blender or food processor and blend until smooth. Add the cayenne pepper oil and the olive oil, a teaspoon at a time, until the sauce is smooth and slightly thickened.

Transfer the sauce to a small stainless-steel saucepan and boil for 2 to 3 minutes over a high heat. Remove the pan from the heat and let the sauce cool slightly. Place in a clean jar and refrigerate. Serve cold or at room temperature. *Makes ½ cup.*

Salsa Picante (*Hot Sauce*)

This Mexican *salsa* is spiked with the fresh, distinctive flavor of fresh coriander. When freshly made, it is hot—as in VERY HOT. The longer it sits the more subdued its fire becomes; it is best served within a few hours. Serve as a dip with taco chips and guacamole or as a condiment with tortillas, grilled meats and eggs.

    4 large, ripe tomatoes, chopped
    3 scallions, thinly sliced
    2 tablespoons chopped fresh coriander leaves
 2½ tablespoons fresh lime juice
    2 fresh jalapeño or serrano chiles, trimmed and chopped
      (with seeds)
    1 large clove garlic, chopped
  ½ cup water
    Salt to taste

In a large bowl, mix the tomatoes, scallions, coriander and lime juice and set aside.

In a blender or food processor, blend the chiles and garlic until finely chopped. Add the water and process for another 2 to 3 seconds until well blended. Add the chile and garlic sauce to the tomato mixture and mix well; add salt to taste. Refrigerate and serve. *Makes about 3 cups.*

Salsa Cruda

This is a really versatile *salsa*. It goes with any type of barbecued food, fried shrimp and chicken or on grilled fish. It also makes a great dip for *nachos* or taco chips with guacamole.

1   cup very ripe fresh tomatoes, coarsely chopped
2   tablespoons fresh lime juice
2   to 3 tablespoons finely chopped jalapeño or serrano chile peppers
1   small onion, coarsely chopped

Mix all the ingredients and let sit an hour. This sauce is best used within 6 hours; the longer it sits, the less intense and crunchy it becomes. *Makes about 1 cup.*

Mission-Style Salsa

I first tasted this incredibly hot *salsa* at a party in New York given for a friend who was leaving for Latin America. Robert Huff sent me his recipe along with the following notes: "Fresh *cilantro* (coriander) is an essential ingredient in this recipe. It provides a cooling, earthy relief from the hot peppers. *Salsa* can be spooned on eggs, steak and barbecued foods. It is most often served as a dip with corn chips or taco chips. *Salsa* is high in vitamin C. In Los Angeles, *salsa*, taco chips and shots of tequilla are touted as being an effective cold remedy. A good *salsa* should always make you sweat." *This recipe makes enough for a crowd.*

10 fresh plum tomatoes, peeled and coarsely chopped
2 cups canned tomatoes, coarsely chopped
8 cloves garlic, minced
2 medium onions, one minced and one coarsely chopped
6 scallions, thinly sliced
1 large green bell pepper, coarsely chopped
3 to 4 fresh green chile peppers, coarsely chopped with seeds
5 jalapeño peppers, coarsely chopped with seeds
8 serrano peppers, coarsely chopped with seeds
¾ cup chopped fresh coriander
½ cup red wine vinegar
¼ cup olive oil
½ teaspoon cayenne pepper
½ teaspoon freshly ground black pepper

Mix all the ingredients in a large bowl and let sit for 30 minutes before serving. *Makes about 6½ cups.*

Brazilian Hot Pepper and Lemon Sauce

This very spicy, very sour sauce is an adaptation of the Brazilian sauce, *Môlho de Pimenta e Limão*. It is traditionally served with *feijoada* (the national dish of Brazil)—a feast of smoked and fresh meats, black beans, Brazilian rice, greens and orange slices. It is also excellent with grilled meats, pork and shrimp. Make the sauce just before serving; it tends to lose its crunchy texture after a few hours.

    5 finely chopped bottled, pickled tabasco peppers, plus ¼
        teaspoon of the vinegar
    ½ cup lemon juice
    1 small onion, finely chopped
    2 cloves garlic, finely chopped
    ¼ cup minced parsley

Mix all the ingredients in a small serving bowl. Let sit, uncovered, at room temperature, for about 15 minutes before serving. *Makes about 1 cup.*

Sherry Peppers Sauce

Flavoring dry sherry with chile peppers is an old Bermudian tradition. In just about every restaurant on the island, small bottles of this hot, spicy condiment are served. You can buy bottled sherry peppers sauce (see page 122), but it's really easy to make your own. If you make this sauce in an old mason jar or glass bottle it makes a great gift.

Use it in soups, chowders, marinades and barbecue sauces or sprinkle over fried eggs and pan-fried fish. A dash of sherry peppers sauce in a rich seafood chowder is an incredible taste sensation. Plan on letting the sauce steep for at least two weeks before using.

    4 fresh red or green chile peppers (you can use any type of
       pepper you want, depending on just how hot you want
       the sauce to be)
    2 small dried red chile peppers
    2 cups dry sherry

Place all of the peppers in a clean, clear bottle or mason jar and cover with the sherry. Seal tightly and let steep for at least two weeks before using. After two weeks, taste the sauce. Be careful, it will be hot—very hot. You can leave the peppers in (which will cause the sauce to get hotter, though not too much hotter) or strain them out at this point. Keep in a dark, cool spot. *Makes 2 cups.*

Freshly Grated Horseradish

Making fresh horseradish can be a painful, tearful, sinus-clearing experience. The traditional way to do it is to grate the fresh horse-radish root by hand. If you choose this method, be sure to have plenty of tissues around. An easier way to make freshly grated horseradish is in a blender or food processor. But this, you should be warned, has its risks, too. Do not stick your head over the blender to see how the horseradish is doing; the fumes from the horseradish root are so intense that a coughing fit is virtually guaranteed. Use a spatula to stir the horseradish around and check on its texture. Now that you've been told of all the possible dangers, enjoy. Freshly grated horseradish is a spicy, pungent treat that is definitely worth the effort.

> 1 cup peeled, diced horseradish (you can use either a peeler or a small, sharp knife to peel the horseradish root)
> About ¼ cup white wine or cider vinegar (never measure vinegar in a metal container; always use a glass or porcelain measuring cup)
> Salt to taste

Place the horseradish in a blender or food processor and blend until thoroughly grated, about 5 to 6 seconds. If you're going to serve the horseradish right away (and if you like it strong and straight), stop here. If, however, you want to store it for future use (and if you like a creamy-style horseradish), add the vinegar to the blender, 1 tablespoon at a time, until it reaches the desired consistency. Taste for seasoning (watch out), and stir in the salt to taste. Place in a small, clear bottle or jar and refrigerate. Use within three to four weeks. *Makes about ½ cup.*

Fresh Horseradish with Beets (Red Horseradish)

Fresh beets not only give horseradish a beautiful pinkish-red color but they also add a delicious, natural sweetness.

Follow the above recipe and add ¼ to ½ cup of freshly cooked diced beets to the blender along with the diced horseradish. *Makes about ¾ cup.*

COOKING WITH HOT PEPPER SAUCES AND HORSERADISH

Swordfish with Horseradish-Thyme Butter

In this recipe, the milk and the natural fish juice create a creamy sauce, and the horseradish butter provides a sharp, spicy contrast.

   1   pound swordfish steak, cut about 1-inch thick
   ½   cup milk
   2½   tablespoons unsalted butter
   1½   tablespoons prepared white horseradish
   1   tablespoon fresh lemon juice
   2   sprigs thyme, or ¼ teaspoon dried thyme
   1   lemon, cut into wedges

Place the swordfish in a small baking pan. Pour the milk over the fish and marinate, covered, for about 1½ hours.

Preheat the oven to 350°. In a small saucepan, melt the butter over moderate heat. Add the horseradish, lemon juice and thyme. Cook, stirring, until slightly thickened, about 3 minutes. Spoon the horseradish butter over the swordfish and bake for 15 minutes, or until just tender when tested with a fork. Place under the broiler until golden brown, bubbling and opaque throughout, about 4 to 5 minutes. Serve with lemon wedges. *Serves 2 to 3.*

Devilish Oysters

These oysters—grilled with hot pepper sauce and a touch of fresh breadcrumbs—make an excellent first course or hors d'oeuvre. Keep the shells after you've shucked the oysters; you may want to serve the oysters in their shells after they've been grilled.

You can use any type of hot pepper sauce or *sambal* you want with this recipe; the Chinese chile sauces on pages 110–11 are particularly good.

> 1 dozen shucked oysters, with 2½ tablespoons of juice
> About ½ to 2 teaspoons of hot pepper sauce
> 1½ teaspoons fresh breadcrumbs

Preheat the broiler. Place the oysters with the juice in a small, shallow casserole or a medium-size, ovenproof skillet. Drizzle a few drops of the hot sauce over each oyster; ½ teaspoon makes the oysters mildly hot and 2 teaspoons is "watch-out" hot. Top each oyster with breadcrumbs and place under the broiler for 4 to 5 minutes, or until cooked and tender.

Place the oysters back in their shells or serve them straight out of the casserole. *Serves 2 to 3.*

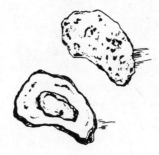

Sour Cream, Horseradish and Caper Sauce

Serve this simple, piquant sauce with smoked fish or smoked ham. It's also delicious with roast beef or as a dip for beef fondue or raw vegetables.

> 1 cup sour cream
> 2 tablespoons freshly grated horseradish, or 3 tablespoons drained bottled horseradish
> 2 tablespoons capers, drained
> 1 teaspoon Tabasco or hot pepper sauce

Mix together the sour cream, horseradish and capers and add the Tabasco to taste. Refrigerate and serve cold. *Makes 1 cup.*

Horseradish Butter

This pungent butter is delicious added to steamed new potatoes, grilled fish or beef. You can make it with either white or red (beet) horseradish, depending on what it's being served with. The bright color of the red horseradish butter is fantastic with pan-fried filet of sole, boiled new potatoes or grilled salmon.

- 1 stick salted butter, at room temperature
- 2 tablespoons freshly grated horseradish, or 3 tablespoons drained prepared horseradish
- 1 teaspoon freshly ground black pepper

Using the back of a wooden spoon, cream the butter until light and fluffy. Stir in the horseradish and pepper.

Spread a tablespoon of flour over your hands and on a clean work surface. Form the butter into a log shape and wrap in wax paper. Refrigerate or freeze and slice off a tablespoon at a time as needed. *Makes ½ cup.*

The Beach Plum Inn's Horseradish Sauce

The Beach Plum Inn, in Menemsha on Martha's Vineyard, Massachusetts, serves this delicious sauce on top of a cold medallion of beef salad. Bibb (or Boston) lettuce leaves are arranged on a serving plate and topped with thinly sliced, slightly rare medallions of beef. The horseradish sauce can be served on top of the beef or on the side.

1   cup heavy cream
3   tablespoons prepared horseradish, drained
2   teaspoons lemon juice
½   teaspoon salt
    About ¼ teaspoon Tabasco sauce
¼   teaspoon white pepper

Whip the cream until it forms peaks. Gently fold in the horseradish, lemon juice, salt, Tabasco and pepper. Taste for seasoning and add additional Tabasco sauce if desired. Refrigerate and serve. *Makes about 1 cup.*

5

OCCIDENTAL
(OR WESTERN) SAUCES

*Ketchup, Mayonnaise, Steak Sauce,
Worcestershire, Cranberry Sauce,
Cumberland Sauce*

OCCIDENTAL SAUCES ARE familiar to most Americans, but their histories are surprisingly exotic. Who would have thought, for instance, that ketchup originated in China, was imported to England and then popularized in the United States? Or that mayonnaise is based on a Spanish garlic sauce and Worcestershire on an ancient Roman recipe?

OCCIDENTAL SAUCE
SURVEY

Over the years, these sauces have become an integral part of the American diet. Most of them are now considered everyday "supermarket sauces," but recently a number of new, updated renditions have surfaced in specialty food shops.

Ketchup

We are a nation in which the average man, woman and child consumes 1¾ gallons of ketchup a year. Americans use ketchup to spice up their hamburgers, hot dogs, french fries, and even their politics. It was only a few years ago that President Ronald Reagan created a national controversy by declaring ketchup a legitimate vegetable for school lunches. The Reagan policy provided a rare opportunity for food critics and welfare mothers to get together on an issue. Both knew the ultimate truth—ketchup is a condiment, *not* a vegetable.

There are several explanations about the derivation of the word "ketchup." Some historians say it was named after *kechap*, a tangy sauce made in Malaysia and Singapore; others claim it comes from the Siamese word *"kachiap"* or the Indonesian word *"ketjáp,"* meaning a sauce added to food for extra flavor. But the most widely accepted story attributes the word to the Chinese. *The Oxford Dictionary of English Etymology* lists the word "ketchup" as early as 1690 and shows it to be of Chinese origin.

The story goes that in the mid-seventeenth century English sailors discovered the Chinese using a pungent sauce made of fish entrails and brine called *ke tsiap*. The sailors had a need for products that would hold up during long sea voyages, and an even stronger need for sauces that would spice up their monotonous diet while on board ship. They took *ke tsiap* back to England. But once they got home and tried to recreate the sauce, the idea of fish entrails seemed less and less appealing. So English cooks experimented with the recipe using more conventional ingredients.

Walnut, oyster and mushroom ketchups were particularly popular. In 1748, Mrs. Harrison wrote in her popular *Housekeeper's Pocketbook* that "no good British homemaker should ever be without the pungent condiment."

Ketchup eventually made its way to the United States in the latter part of the seventeenth century. It is said that cooks from Maine were the first to invent a tomato-based ketchup. Maine sea captains who traveled to Mexico and the Spanish West Indies brought tomato seeds back with them and planted the seeds with great success. The result was a spicy, pungent sauce that is still served throughout New England with baked beans, fish cakes and meat.

Before tomato ketchup caught on across the whole country, there were a number of other ketchups that characterized early American cooking. Regional cooks made the popular sauce using whatever ingredients happened to be in abundance. The early Shakers, for instance, made ketchup from apples, cucumbers, gooseberries and grapes.

In 1861, Isabella Beeton wrote in her popular guide, *Mrs. Beeton's Book of Household Management,* "This flavoring, if genuine and well prepared, is one of the most useful sauces to the experienced cook, and no trouble should be spared in its preparation." Up until the late 1800s, it was commonplace for American housewives to spend hours over a hot wood stove simmering up pots of homemade ketchup.

Then in 1876, Mr. Henry Heinz had a brainstorm. The rest is history. Ketchup is now commercially made and consumed the world over, but it is ultimately considered an all-American condiment.

TASTING NOTES:
Americans love to eat ketchup with just about everything. Hamburgers and french fries are traditional, but ketchup also gets poured onto hot dogs, steaks, chops—even baked potatoes.

We tend to think of ketchup as an ordinary, everyday sauce, but when I was in France a few years ago I was amazed to find it in some of the finest specialty food shops. It seems that in some parts of France, ketchup is being marketed as a kind of trendy American sauce. At *The Ritz Hotel* in Paris, the head chef makes an elegant sweetbread and vegetable salad served with a ketchup-based vinaigrette.

Ketchup is delicious in baked beans, stews, as a base for barbecue sauce (see page 165 for recipe), marinades and spicy cocktail sauces. A tablespoon of ketchup whisked into a vinaigrette is wonderful served with ripe red tomatoes and thick slices of red onion.

BEST BRANDS:

Most of the commercially produced ketchups you find in grocery stores are loaded with sweeteners and thickeners. But there are now a number of small companies that produce "salt-free," "sugar-free" and "all natural" ketchup. They tend to cost a bit more, but they're usually worth it. Best of all is homemade ketchup; see recipes on pages 159–60.

Casa Peña Blanca Texas Ketchup—Made in El Paso, Texas, this is exactly what you'd expect from something called "Texas ketchup." It's a tomato-based sauce electrified with green chiles, ground jalapeño chiles, onions, vinegar, mustard and spices. It's fantastic on burgers and french fries or as a dip for boiled shrimp or crab.

Gathering Winds All Natural Ketchup—Made without sugar, salt or any preservatives, this ketchup has a surprisingly good taste. We've been so conditioned to believe that if ketchup isn't thick, it isn't good. Well, this ketchup disproves that myth once and for all. Made in Ithaca, New York, from tomatoes, organic apple cider vinegar, unfiltered honey and spices, it's a truly good ketchup.

Geo Watkins Mushroom Ketchup—This thick, rich, mushroomy ketchup was considered "the secret sauce of many Victorian cooks." Made in England, it is the perfect accompaniment to old English favorites like steak and kidney pie, grilled kidney, lamb chops or savory puddings. It gives the word "ketchup" a whole new meaning.

Geo Watkins Walnut Ketchup—Once upon a time, walnut ketchup was all the rage in England; once you taste this ketchup, you'll understand why. Made from black walnuts, anchovies, malt vinegar and spices, it has the consistency of Worcestershire sauce and a rich, unique flavor. Serve with steaks, grilled lamb chops, roasts, grilled fish and in soups and sauces. Use it to deglaze the pan juices from a sautéed chop or steak.

Heinz Ketchup—I grew up on this sauce so it will probably always have a place in my refrigerator. Obviously, I'm not alone. Heinz sells more than 300 million bottles of ketchup in the United States every year. It's thick, rich and delicious.

Lifespice Tomato Velvet—Lifespice, a New York-based company,

[148]

is dedicated to making salt-free condiments and sauces. This thick, rich, tomatoey ketchup is superb. Made without "salt, preservatives or anything artificial," it's delicious on hamburgers, in pasta sauces or mixed with yogurt and spread on oven-baked fish.

Old San Antonio's Jalapeño Catsup—Ooo-la-la. The spicy, biting flavor of jalapeño peppers gives this ketchup a whole new dimension. It's spicy without being destructive. And it's full of good, fresh tomato flavor. Excellent on burgers.

Walnut Acres Ketchup—Made from organically grown tomatoes and onions, homemade apple cider vinegar, honey and spices, this is a tart, pungent ketchup. Its slightly spicy flavor is great with fried chicken, fried zucchini and in pasta sauces.

Mayonnaise

There are few sauces considered more American than mayonnaise. But, like many American foods, this egg-and-oil-based sauce has its roots in an old European recipe. There are several theories about the origin of mayonnaise, the most popular being that it is based on *alioli*, a Spanish garlic sauce that dates back hundreds of years.

It is believed that sometime in the seventeenth century, French cardinal and statesman Richelieu visited Mahón, the capital of the Balearic island of Minorca, and tasted *alioli*. He was so impressed by the garlic sauce that he brought the recipe back to France. There, French chefs experimented with the sauce, eliminating the garlic and replacing it with the tart, lighter flavor of fresh lemon juice. They named their creation *sauce Mahónnaise*, but in time it was changed to mayonnaise.

Exactly when mayonnaise made its way to the United States isn't clearly documented, but it has been commercially manufactured in this country for quite some time. Inside a stack of old cookbooks I bought at a country auction a few years ago, I found a calendar and recipe booklet, published by the Hellmann's Mayonnaise Com-

[149]

pany, that dates back to 1926. The calendar is filled with wonderful vintage recipes like Tutti-Frutti salad, jellied vegetable mold and (get this) peanut butter and olive sandwiches with mayonnaise. But the best part of the calendar is the introduction: "Mayonnaise dressing has been known for centuries . . . Ever since it was first made, mayonnaise has been considered a great delicacy and one which required a great skill and art and patience to prepare successfully at home. . . ."

I was amazed to see that, as early as 1926, Americans were being "brainwashed" into believing that making mayonnaise at home is a time-consuming and difficult task. Granted, bottled mayonnaise was seen by many as a time-saving convenience but, over the years, it has come to mean a mediocre, fairly tasteless condiment. The fact of the matter is that it's incredibly easy to make delicious, fresh-tasting mayonnaise; see recipe on page 161.

TASTING NOTES:
Serve mayonnaise with sandwiches and cold meat platters, in salads and coleslaw. Use as the base for flavored sauces; see pages 162–63 for ideas. You can also use homemade mayonnaise to make tartar sauce; see recipe on page 164.

Although nothing can beat a homemade mayonnaise, there are now a number of sauces sold in supermarkets, health food stores and specialty food shops that are worth mentioning.

BEST BRANDS:
Benedicta Mayonnaise—This French-made sauce, which is sold in tubes, is rich and creamy. It's wonderful on sandwiches and for decorating savory pastries and hors d'oeuvres. This is the perfect mayonnaise to bring on a picnic.

Hain's Saf-flower Mayonnaise—This light, smooth mayonnaise is made (as the name suggests) with safflower oil, eggs, cider vinegar, natural honey and lemon juice. It contains no preservatives and can be found in health food stores.

Hellmann's (called *Best Foods* in the West)—In 1913 Richard

Hellmann began making mayonnaise on a commercial basis and to this day it is one of America's favorites. I grew up on this mayonnaise so I suppose I'm prejudiced, but I do believe it's the best supermarket brand available. Add a touch of lemon juice and it gives this mayonnaise a fresh, delicious flavor.

Walnut Acres Mayonnaise—The folks at this natural foods farm in Penns Creek, Pennsylvania, claim that their customers say this mayonnaise is "the nicest, best-flavored, most wholesome product they have ever found." It's made fresh with whole eggs, safflower oil, apple cider vinegar, alfalfa honey, mustard and spices. Walnut Acres also makes a *Salt-Free Mayonnaise*. They are both delicious.

Steak Sauces

The popularity of Worcestershire sauce (see page 153) in the mid-1800s inspired many variations, most of which were sauces created to be served with steak. I have never understood the appeal of steak sauce. Buying an expensive cut of beef and then pouring a sweet, gloppy sauce over it just doesn't make sense to me. Obviously there are a lot of people who disagree; steak sauce is a big seller almost everywhere.

BEST BRANDS:
The classic American steak sauces you find in coffee shops and cheap steak houses all taste about the same to me. Among the better one's I've tried are *A.1. Steak Sauce* and *Heinz 57 Sauce*. I wouldn't use them on a steak but on a burger—well, maybe. What's far more interesting (and delicious) are some of the new varieties of steak sauces now being sold in specialty food stores across the country. Listed below are a few of my favorites:

Elsenham's The Gentleman's Sauce—This is like a thick, sweet-and-sour ketchup. It's excellent with beef, fried eggs, grilled chops and hamburgers. Made in England, the sauce is based on an old English recipe that's been popular since 1828.

Jamaican Choice Hot Pepper Sauce—Although they call this a hot pepper sauce, it's really more of a spicy steak sauce. Made in Costa Rica from crushed peppers, vinegar and spices, it is a thick, dark-red sauce that goes well with all sorts of grilled or barbecued meats and poultry.

Lea & Perrins HP Steak Sauce—Created by the people who make the world-famous Worcestershire sauce, this is the quintessential British steak sauce. According to the label it's been "the world's largest selling steak sauce for over half a century." HP is a thick, dark-brown sauce with a nice balance of sweet-and-sour flavors. The key ingredients are dates, vinegar, molasses, tomato paste, tamarind, raisins, onions and garlic. It's delicious served with a mixed English grill or a simple broiled lamb chop.

Old San Antonio Salsa Tampiqueña—This Mexican steak sauce is hot, hot, hot—a surefire way to wake up any steak. Made from tomatoes, jalapeño peppers, onions, vinegar and spices, it is a thick, spicy sauce that is fantastic with grilled steak or chops. I'd choose this over the ordinary American-style steak sauces any day.

OX-1 Sesame Steak Sauce—"In the heart of Osaka, Japan, stands the dream of Madame Yoko, the internationally famous OX-1 Steak House. OX-1 Sesame Steak Sauce is the pride of Madame Yoko. A tasteful remembrance of the mystery of Japan." That's the story told on the label of this outrageously good Japanese steak sauce. Made with sesame seeds, *mirin* (a sweet Japanese rice wine), soy sauce, tomato puree, vinegar and spices, this mixture gives steak sauce a whole new definition. The bits of ground sesame seeds give the sauce a great texture. Serve it with grilled chicken, steaks, fish or vegetables. It's also delicious as a dip for dumplings, barbecued ribs or fried chicken.

Peter Luger Steak House Old Fashioned Sauce—As far as I'm concerned, Peter Luger Steak House in Brooklyn, New York, is the best in the United States. Aside from having the absolutely tenderest, most buttery steaks, they also happen to make a great steak sauce. At the restaurant, it's served with a plate of thickly sliced ripe red tomatoes and raw onions; it also goes beautifully with grilled steak. For years it was only sold at the restaurant, but it is now available at some specialty food shops. It's a thick, tomato-based sauce spiced with horseradish, soy sauce, tamarind, anchovies, molasses, onions, garlic and spices. Serve with steaks, hamburgers, grilled chops, grilled chicken or with salads. It also makes a great dipping sauce for cold shrimp.

Pickapeppa Sauce—Made in Shooters Hill, Jamaica, this is a thick, sweet, piquant sauce. Although it's touted as being a hot pepper sauce, there really isn't anything particularly spicy about it. Made from tomatoes, tamarind, onions, raisins, vinegar and spices, it goes well with steaks, grilled chops and roasts; it's also delicious in soups, stews and sauces.

Sharwood's London Steak Sauce—"Originally made in England during the reign of King George IV," says the label, this thick, ketchup-like steak sauce has a terrific flavor. Made with tomatoes, dates, fruit and spices, it's delicious with steaks, prime rib, burgers and curries.

Wan Ja Shan Hot Chinese-Style Steak Sauce—Made in China, this is a delicious, slightly spicy sauce that is fantastic with stir-fried beef and vegetables. It also goes well with steaks and chops and as a dipping sauce for vegetables and fried fish, too.

Worcestershire Sauce

It's black and rich, pungent and salty. Its flavor is almost meaty, but there's also a slight hint of fish. It tastes as good in a Bloody Mary as it does on a hamburger. Most people can't spell it, but almost everyone has tried it. It is, in a word, unique.

Worcestershire sauce has been popular since the 1830s. But just how old the recipe is, no one is exactly sure. A variation of Worcestershire is said to date back to the ancient Romans, who made a sauce of salted fish called *garum*.

The people at Lea & Perrins (makers of the world's best-selling Worcestershire sauce) have their own explanation about the origins of Worcestershire. Their story goes something like this: In 1830, Lord Sandys, Governor General of Bengal, discovered a recipe for a pungent Indian sauce and brought it back to England. He gave the recipe to two druggists, John Lea and William Perrins. They tasted the sauce and found it to be absolutely awful so they immediately dumped the sauce into a few wooden barrels in their basement and forgot all about it. Years later, they remembered the sauce and went downstairs to discard it. But first, they decided to give it another taste. And, lo and behold, this awful concoction had developed a fantastic flavor.

Lea & Perrins named the sauce Worcestershire because it was made in the shire of Worcester. Since the sauce kept so well and actually developed flavor as it aged, it became popular on board ships. Sailors used liberal amounts of the sauce to disguise the rancid taste of their food. Before long, Worcestershire sauce became popular worldwide.

Today *Lea & Perrins Worcestershire Sauce* is made using the chemists' original recipe. Anchovies, soybeans, tamarind, vinegar, garlic, shallots, molasses and spices are mixed in enormous wooden vats. The sauce is allowed to age for two years before being pressed and strained. It is then placed in its distinctive glass bottle and wrapped in the traditional Lea & Perrins brown paper.

TASTING NOTES:
Worcestershire sauce adds a great flavor to marinades and other sauces, but it's best used as a table condiment. Splash it on burgers and steaks, eggs, fried fish, baked clams and grilled cheese sandwiches.

Lea & Perrins is the most famous, but there are also a number of other good brands of Worcestershire sauce available:

BEST BRANDS:

Barbecue Brand Worcestershire Sauce—This sauce comes from London, where it's been made by Keddie, Ltd., since 1857. It has a good, sweet, tangy flavor, but ultimately it can't compare to Lea & Perrins.

Bull Dog Worcestershire—This is a very sweet, Japanese-made Worcestershire sauce. It doesn't have much bite, but it does add a good flavor to fried eggs, soups and stews.

Sharwood's Worcestershire Sauce—Made in England, this is a delicious, slightly salty Worcestershire. It's particularly good in soups, stews and other sauces.

Other Occidental Sauces

Cranberry Sauce is an American tradition. I love it, but wonder why it is that we only eat it at holiday time. See page 157 for a recipe you can make when fresh cranberries are in season and then freeze and enjoy year-round.

Cumberland Sauce is a sweet, slightly spicy mixture of red currant jelly, dry port wine, oranges and spices. According to Elizabeth David's *Spices, Salts and Aromatics in the English Kitchen,* "[Cumberland sauce] was named after Ernest, Duke of Cumberland," and is "probably German in origin."

The sauce became popular in England in the early 1800s. Initially, it was found only in the kitchens of the aristocracy but was soon made popular by the famous French chef Auguste Escoffier. Cumberland sauce was originally created to be served with boar's head, but it also goes well with more common foods like roast lamb, beef, venison, ham and tongue. *Fortnum & Mason* of London makes a wonderful Cumberland sauce, but the best is homemade; see recipe on page 158.

In eighteenth-century England, dozens of new sauces were created to improve the flavor of meats, game and fish. *Harvey Sauce* was reputedly invented by Peter Harvey, host of the Black Dog Inn in Middlesex. The main ingredients are anchovies, walnut pickles, soy sauce, malt vinegar, garlic and spices. Like its rival, Worcestershire sauce, Harvey's is aged for several years and then strained to create a clear, rich sauce.

Harvey sauce never caught on in the United States the way it did in England. There are now, however, several brands of the sauce sold in American specialty food shops. *Geo Watkins* of London makes a particularly good Harvey sauce. It's a dark, fairly thin condiment that is delicious in soups and stews and served with meats, game and poultry.

Mint Sauce is another British favorite. It is traditionally served with leg of lamb, lamb chops or grilled butterflied lamb. But mint sauce is also wonderful with roast beef, pork, chicken, ground lamb burgers and curries. (See page 212 for information on mint jellies.)

Mint sauce is easy to make: Simply place ½ cup finely chopped fresh mint in a bowl or jar. Boil ⅓ cup white wine vinegar in a stainless-steel pan with 1 tablespoon of white or brown sugar. Pour over the mint and let sit for 2 to 3 hours before serving.

A number of good commercially made mint sauces are sold in this country. *Elsenham* makes a delicious sauce, thick with chopped fresh mint. According to the label, it's "impossible to imagine roast lamb without this product of English gardens." *HP Mint Sauce* is another fresh-tasting condiment. It's like a thick, mint puree and can be diluted with vinegar and sugar according to taste.

Muscadine Sauce is a deliciously sweet, slightly smokey flavored sauce. It's made from muscadine grapes, which are native to the eastern and southern United States. *The Callaway Gardens Country Store* in Pine Mountain, Georgia, makes a delicious muscadine sauce. Use it as a glaze for pork, duck or chicken, or as a dipping sauce for spareribs, fried chicken and shrimp. It's also superb spooned over pancakes, crepes, ice cream and pies.

MAKING YOUR OWN
OCCIDENTAL SAUCES

Lucy's Cranberry-Orange-Maple Sauce

Make this delicious sauce in the fall, when cranberries are in season, and then freeze it so you can enjoy it year-round.

Serve with roast turkey, chicken, duck or ham, or spooned over baked or pureed squash. It's also delicious with ice cream and butter cookies.

- 1 cup, plus 2 tablespoons white sugar
- 2 cups water
- 1 pound fresh cranberries, about 4 cups
- ⅓ cup freshly squeezed orange juice
- ¼ cup maple syrup
- 1 tablespoon grated orange rind
- 1 tablespoon coarsely chopped candied ginger, or ¼ teaspoon grated fresh ginger

In a large saucepan, mix the sugar with the water and simmer over moderately high heat for about 5 minutes, or until the liquid becomes slightly syrupy. Add the cranberries and simmer another 5 minutes, or until the berries begin to pop open. Add the orange juice, maple syrup, orange rind and ginger and simmer another 2 to 3 minutes.

Pour the sauce into hot, sterilized jars and place in the refrigerator or freezer. *Makes about 5 cups.*

Cumberland Sauce

  1 cup red currant or black currant jelly
  2 tablespoons very thinly sliced orange rind
  2 tablespoons orange juice
  1 tablespoon sugar
1½ teaspoons powdered mustard
  ¾ teaspoon ground ginger
  ⅛ teaspoon salt
  ⅛ teaspoon black pepper
  ½ cup dry port

Heat the jelly, orange rind and juice, sugar, mustard, ginger, salt and pepper in a saucepan over a moderate heat for 5 minutes. Stir occasionally to dissolve the mustard and ginger. Add the port and let simmer for 5 to 10 minutes, or until slightly thickened. Let cool and refrigerate. Serve cold. *Makes about 1½ cups.*

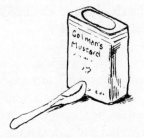

Homemade Tomato Ketchup

You'll need lots of fresh, ripe tomatoes for this ketchup. The best time to make this is in August, when your garden (or your local farmer's market) is overflowing with ripe, inexpensive tomatoes. This ketchup takes some time to make but the results are definitely worth it; you may never use bottled ketchup again.

    10 pounds ripe tomatoes, chopped
     1 large red onion, thinly sliced
     1 cup apple cider vinegar
    ¾ to 1 cup brown or white sugar
     2 tablespoons salt
     1 teaspoon cayenne pepper
     1 teaspoon ground cinnamon
     1 teaspoon ground allspice
     1 teaspoon baking soda
    ¼ teaspoon freshly grated nutmeg

Place the tomatoes and the onion in a large stainless-steel saucepan and place over a moderate heat for 30 minutes, or until the tomatoes are soft and have broken down. Strain the mixture through a large sieve, making sure to stir as much of the pulp through as possible. (Don't worry if the liquid seems very watery; it will thicken later.)

Place the strained tomatoes back into the saucepan and whisk in the remaining ingredients. Let the mixture simmer over a moderate heat for 1½ to 2 hours, stirring occasionally, until the mixture has thickened to the consistency of ketchup. Place into sterilized mason jars and refrigerate; it will keep for several months. If you want to double the recipe and preserve the ketchup, process in a boiling water bath for 20 minutes (see page 216 for additional notes on canning). *Makes 4 to 6 cups.*

Quick Ketchup

This slightly spicy ketchup, created by Penny Potenz Winship of New York City, is terrific for people who are watching their weight or their sodium intake. It is made in the blender without salt or sugar and tastes as good (if not better) than anything you'll ever find in the stores. If tightly covered and refrigerated, it will keep for months.

    1 medium onion, chopped (about 1 cup)
   ½ clove of garlic
   5 tablespoons frozen apple juice concentrate
   1 can (6 ounces) tomato paste
   ½ cup malt vinegar
   ½ teaspoon cayenne pepper
   ¼ teaspoon ground cinnamon
   ⅛ teaspoon ground cloves

Place the onion, garlic and apple juice concentrate in the blender and purée until smooth. Add the remaining ingredients and blend until smooth. Keep in an airtight bottle or jar and refrigerate. *Makes about 1 cup.*

Basic Homemade Mayonnaise

There have been volumes written about the "best" recipe for mayonnaise (some claiming that it *must* be made from olive oil, others arguing that it has to be a light vegetable oil). I have no intention of adding to that long-running debate. The point is to start making your own mayonnaise at home; it's cheap, easy and tastes a lot better than most bottled varieties.

Many people like to make mayonnaise in a blender or food processor. I've always preferred to make mayonnaise with a whisk or a hand-held electric beater so that I can watch the process. You have a lot more control over the texture and consistency of your mayonnaise if you can see it thicken, bit by bit.

Use whatever type of oil you like with this recipe. I prefer a richly flavored mayonnaise and use either all olive oil or ¾ cup olive oil and ¼ cup light vegetable oil. Whatever you choose, make sure all your ingredients (plus your bowl and whisk) are at room temperature. If your ingredients are too hot or cold the sauce won't hold together.

> 2 egg yolks, at room temperature
> 1 teaspoon Dijon mustard
> 1½ tablespoons lemon juice
> ½ teaspoon salt
> ¼ teaspoon pepper, preferably white
> 1 cup olive, peanut, safflower or vegetable oil
> 1 tablespoon white wine vinegar

In a large bowl, whisk the egg yolks by hand or with an electric beater until they begin to thicken slightly and turn a light lemon color. Whisk in the mustard, 1 tablespoon of the lemon juice, and the salt and pepper. Gradually add ½ cup of the oil, a few drops at a time, making sure that each drop has been incorporated before adding the next.

At this stage, the sauce should begin to thicken and hold to-

[161]

gether. You can relax and add the additional ½ cup of oil in a *slow*, steady stream. When almost all the oil has been added, whisk in the vinegar and the remaining ½ tablespoon of the lemon juice. Taste for seasoning and adjust, if needed. If the mayonnaise doesn't seem to be holding together, add a tablespoon of boiling water and whisk until the sauce comes together. (See note for further hints.) Don't be concerned if the mayonnaise seems a bit thin, it will thicken a bit in the refrigerator. Refrigerate the mayonnaise in a glass jar or covered bowl for at least a few hours before serving; use within 5 days. *Makes 1 cup.*

Note: If your mayonnaise begins to separate, don't panic. There's a simple way to save it: whisk an egg yolk in a bowl until it turns a light lemon color. Then, gradually whisk into the separated mayonnaise until the sauce thickens and holds together.

Flavored Mayonnaise

Once you've mastered the basic recipe for mayonnaise you can make all sorts of wonderful sauces. Listed here are a few of my favorites.

Lemon-Curry Mayonnaise: To 1 cup of homemade mayonnaise, whisk in 2 tablespoons lemon juice, 2 teaspoons curry powder and 1 teaspoon cumin powder. Serve with a shrimp and potato salad, a cold mussel or tuna salad or a cold beef and scallion salad. It's also delicious on a cold lamb sandwich or with deviled eggs.

Green Herb Mayonnaise: When making the basic mayonnaise recipe, substitute 1 tablespoon herb-flavored vinegar for the white wine vinegar. To 1 cup homemade mayonnaise, stir in ¾ cup finely chopped assorted fresh herbs (tarragon, basil, opal basil, chives, rosemary, parsley or thyme). Serve with a cold seafood salad, poached salmon, cold pasta salad, chicken salad or on a sandwich of ripe tomato slices and red onion on dark rye bread.

Garlic Mayonnaise: To 1 cup of homemade mayonnaise, add 4 to 6 cloves of garlic mashed with ¼ teaspoon salt and 1 tablespoon fresh lemon juice. Serve with a cold seafood salad, grilled shrimp, mixed vegetable salad, fish stew, roast beef and roasted chicken.

Mustard Mayonnaise: To 1 cup homemade mayonnaise, whisk in ¼ cup strong Dijon mustard. Serve on sandwiches, with cold meat salads, turkey salad, cold tongue and in coleslaw.

Sesame-Ginger Mayonnaise: To 1 cup homemade mayonnaise, mix in 2 teaspoons Oriental sesame oil and 1 tablespoon grated fresh ginger. Use with chicken, turkey or shrimp salad, as a dip for raw vegetables and grilled shrimp, or on a sliced chicken and tomato sandwich.

Horseradish Mayonnaise: To 1 cup homemade mayonnaise, add 2½ tablespoons prepared horseradish. If you like it hotter, add an additional ½ tablespoon. Horseradish with grated beets gives the mayonnaise a beautiful reddish-pink color. Serve with potato salad, coleslaw, cold roast beef and lamb, and with sandwiches.

Lime Mayonnaise: When making the basic mayonnaise recipe, substitute 2 tablespoons fresh lime juice for the lemon juice and vinegar. Serve this mayonnaise with baked salmon, grilled swordfish, cold boiled shrimp or in a turkey or chicken sandwich.

Nut Oil Mayonnaise: To 1 cup homemade mayonnaise, add 1½ to 2 tablespoons walnut, hazelnut or almond oil. Serve with sandwiches and in salads.

Tartar Sauce

I have never tasted a bottled tartar sauce I thought was really terrific. However, it's easy to make. Serve this sauce with fried clams, oysters or fish filets.

    1   cup mayonnaise, preferably homemade
    1½ tablespoons tarragon-flavored vinegar, or white wine
        vinegar
    ½   tablespoon lemon juice
    ½   cup finely chopped pickles or *cornichons* (see page 209
        for explanation)
    4   tablespoons minced onions
    2   tablespoons capers, drained
    1½ tablespoons minced parsley
    1   tablespoon finely chopped chives
    1   teaspoon powdered mustard
    ¼   teaspoon salt
    ⅛   teaspoon cayenne pepper
    1   hard-boiled egg, finely chopped, optional

In a medium bowl, mix the mayonnaise with the remaining ingredients. Stir well to make sure that the mustard is thoroughly dissolved. Refrigerate and serve cold. *Makes about 1½ cups.*

COOKING WITH OCCIDENTAL SAUCES

Bill Bell's Barbecue Sauce

This is a quick, easy barbecue sauce that is delicious with chicken, steak, ribs, or even tofu. You can make it as hot and spicy as you want; add the Tabasco to taste.

1 cup homemade tomato ketchup (see page 159 or 160), or 1 cup of bottled ketchup
About 1 tablespoon Tabasco or other hot pepper sauce to taste
3 tablespoons honey or maple syrup
1½ tablespoons minced fresh garlic

In a large bowl, mix all the ingredients. Taste for seasoning; if you want a very hot sauce, add an additional tablespoon of Tabasco. Add to chicken, meat or tofu; let marinate for a few hours and barbecue.

Marinated Chicken Liver, Apricot and Prune Kebabs

This ketchup-based marinade adds an incredibly good flavor to chicken livers, apricots and prunes. Serve these savory kebabs on triangles of buttered toast as a first course or an hors d'oeuvre.

(You can also use this marinade with steak, lamb or chicken. Triple the recipe and let the meat or poultry marinate for about an hour and then broil or barbecue.)

THE MARINADE

- 2 tablespoons ketchup
- 1 tablespoon Worcestershire sauce
- 1 tablespoon vegetable oil
- 2 teaspoons Dijon mustard
- 2 teaspoons anchovy paste

THE KEBABS

- 12 chicken livers, about ½ pound, cut in half
- 12 dried apricots
- 12 pitted prunes
- 12 slices of bacon, about ¾ pound, each cut into 4 pieces
- 24 bay leaves

In a small bowl, combine the marinade ingredients. Add the livers, toss, and allow to marinate for about 1 hour.

Meanwhile, place the apricots and prunes in a small saucepan with water to cover. Over high heat, bring the water to a boil; reduce heat and poach the fruit until tender but not mushy, about 2 to 3 minutes. Drain, cool and cut each piece of fruit in half.

Preheat the broiler. Wrap each piece of fruit in a section of bacon. Dip the bay leaves in the marinade. Onto each of twelve 7-inch skewers, thread 1 wrapped apricot, 1 bay leaf, 1 piece of chicken liver and a wrapped prune, followed by another apricot, bay leaf, chicken liver and prune. Broil the kebabs about 4 inches from the heat for 2 minutes on each side, or until the bacon is crisp. *Serves 4 to 6.*

Chicken Salad in a Curry-Chutney Mayonnaise with Grapes and Almonds

THE MAYONNAISE

1½ cups homemade mayonnaise (see recipe on page 161)
2 tablespoons mango chutney, finely chopped (see recipe on page 241)
1 tablespoon curry powder
⅛ teaspoon ground cumin
⅛ teaspoon cayenne pepper
1 tablespoon dry white wine
1 tablespoon lemon juice
Salt and pepper to taste

THE SALAD

1 roasted or poached chicken, about 3½ pounds
1 tablespoon unsalted butter
1 cup slivered almonds (4 ounces)
1 pound seedless green grapes
1 bunch watercress

Make the mayonnaise: In a medium-size bowl, mix all the ingredients for the mayonnaise and taste for seasoning. Add additional salt or pepper if needed. Cover and refrigerate until needed.

Prepare the chicken: Separate the meat from the bones and remove the skin, if desired. Slice the chicken into thin strips and set aside.

In a small skillet, melt the butter over moderate heat. Add the almonds and sauté until golden brown, about 4 to 5 minutes. Drain on paper towel and set aside.

Assemble the salad: In a large bowl, mix the chicken slices with ¾ of the mayonnaise, adding more mayonnaise if the salad seems dry. Gently stir in the sautéed almonds and half of the grapes.

Place the salad on a large serving plate and surround with the watercress and remaining grapes. Serve with buttered toast and any remaining mayonnaise on the side. *Serves 4.*

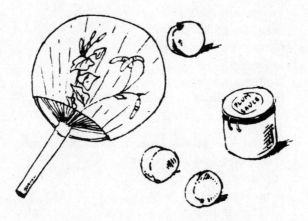

6

ORIENTAL SAUCES

Soy Sauce, Tamari, Hoisin *Sauce*,
Oyster Sauce, Satay *Sauce*

ALTHOUGH CHINESE CUISINE differs greatly from Japanese, just as Thai does from Indonesian, there is one common characteristic that links all Oriental cuisines. It is the idea of contrasting and balancing tastes and textures—what the Chinese call *yin* and *yang*. This philosophy permeates all facets of Eastern culture and in Oriental cooking it's expressed in many ways—hot and sour, crisp and gelatinous, sweet and sour.

Oriental sauces are also created with this philosophy in mind. A sweet-and-sour plum sauce provides flavor and contrast to a garlicky shrimp dish. The pungent taste of Chinese oyster sauce highlights the almost bland flavor of stir-fried lettuce. A smooth, citrus-flavored soy sauce adds sharp contrast to Japanese-style boiled beef with vegetables.

Oriental sauces are used to accentuate the natural flavors of food, not to conceal or overwhelm them. And they are an essential part of a wide variety of Oriental dishes. Some of these sauces are well known to Western cooks; others are exotic and unfamiliar. Experiment with all of them. You'll find that they add an incredibly good flavor to both Eastern and Western dishes.

ORIENTAL SAUCE SURVEY

Fish Sauce: Southeast Asia

Twenty-five hundred years ago the Chinese created a dark, salty sauce made of fermented fish. Years later, soybeans were substituted for fish. While soy sauce went on to become the most widely used condiment in China and Japan, fish sauce remains a staple flavoring ingredient throughout Southeast Asia. It is known by several names, including *patis, nuoc nam, nam pla* and *sauce de poisson.*

Fish sauce is made from fresh anchovies, fish or shrimp layered with salt in huge wooden barrels. This mixture is allowed to ferment for up to eight months. The very best fish sauce, which is the first sauce taken from the barrel, is clear and light brown in color. It's used, almost exclusively, as a table condiment and is the most expensive type of fish sauce. Lower quality (and less expensive) fish sauces come from the bottom of the barrel; these thicker, heavier sauces are used primarily for cooking.

TASTING NOTES:
Fish sauce is a bit of an acquired taste. A friend of mine once described its flavor as being like "rotten anchovies turned into liquid." I wouldn't go that far. Used in moderation, fish sauce provides a subtle, salty fish flavor to soups, stews and marinades. It is frequently used as a seafood dipping sauce (see recipe on page 196). It's also good with Oriental noodle dishes and grilled seafood shish kebab. Fish sauce can be used the same way as soy sauce, but remember that it has a very strong flavor—a little bit goes a long way.

BEST BRANDS:
The following products are all top quality:

Fish Sauce—Made in Hong Kong by the Fishgravy Company.
Lee Seng Heng Fish Sauce—Another favorite from Hong Kong.
Lighthouse Brand Fish Sauce—Made in Singapore.
Lorenzana Patis (Fish Sauce)—Made in the Philippines.
Ruang Tong Brand—Made in Thailand.
Squid Brand Fish Sauce—One of the best Vietnamese fish sauces on the market.
Tiparos Sauce de Poisson (Fish Sauce)—Made in Bangkok.

Hoisin *Sauce: Chinese* (*Chinese Barbecue or Peking Sauce*)

It is mahogany colored, has a thick consistency and a slightly sweet, spicy, almost smokey flavor. Made from mashed and fermented soybeans, garlic, chile peppers, spices and flour, *hoisin* sauce has a unique way of highlighting the natural flavors in food, without drowning them out of existence.

Hoisin sauce is sometimes used in the preparation of Chinese dishes, but it is most often served as a condiment and dipping sauce. It is also called Chinese barbecue sauce because of the way it complements barbecued meats and poultry. *Hoisin* sauce also goes by the name Peking sauce, because it is the traditional condiment served with Peking duck, one of the most sophisticated and spectacular of all Chinese dishes.

Anyone who has ever had the pleasure of eating suckling pig in a really fine Chinese restaurant knows about the capabilities of *hoisin* sauce. Traditionally, the whole, freshly cooked pig is brought to the table for everyone to admire. Then the waiter brings the pig back into the kitchen where the chef skillfully slices the crisp, crackling skin into small squares and then reassembles them back onto the pig's flesh. The first course consists of the crisp pig skin, served with small squares of steamed bread, slivers of fresh scallion and a bowl of *hoisin* sauce. (The *hoisin* helps to "cut" the greasiness of the pig skin.) A "sandwich" is prepared in which the pig skin, scallion and a generous dab of *hoisin* sauce are placed between the hot bread. It is an unforgettable taste sensation.

TASTING NOTES:
Hoisin sauce can be used in marinades (it's particularly good with spareribs) and as a dipping sauce for meats and fish. It's delicious served with shellfish, duck and chicken. A touch of sesame oil mixed into the *hoisin* sauce adds a really nice flavor; serve it with Peking pancakes or barbecued duck or chicken.

BEST BRANDS:
The following brands of Chinese *hoisin* sauce are all highly recommended:

Koon Chun Sauce Factory's Hoisin Sauce
Wan Ja Shan Hoisin Sauce
Yee's Hoisin Sauce

Lemon Sauce: Chinese

Made from lemons, sugar and water, this is a thick, jamlike sauce. Because of its tart, sweet flavor, the Chinese like to serve it as a condiment with duck and chicken. Diluted with a bit of cold water, it makes a great dipping sauce for slightly cooked, still-crisp vegetables. It can also be spread on toast like lemon jam.

BEST BRAND:
Koon Chun Sauce Factory makes a particularly good lemon sauce.

Oyster Sauce: Chinese

The small fishing village at Lau Fah Shan on the South China Sea in Hong Kong is famous for its oysters. Walking through the narrow, open-air seafood market, you see baskets of fresh shellfish being hauled in from the beach. These oysters are not the familiar variety found in American waters, *Ostrea edulis*, but a larger species, *Cassotred gigas*. They are close to three or four inches long, almost the size of a child's shoe. At Lau Fah Shan, young boys spend their entire days, with chisels and long spikes in hand, opening the enormous shells. These oysters are never eaten raw; they are primarily used to make the prized Cantonese condiment, oyster sauce.

This thick, velvety brown sauce is made from dried oysters that are pounded with soy sauce, salt and other seasonings and then fermented in porcelain crocks for several years; the best oyster sauces are allowed to ferment for up to seven or eight years.

TASTING NOTES:
You don't have to be wild about oysters to like oyster sauce. It doesn't taste fishy. It is rich, pungent and somewhat salty, intensifying the natural flavors of food without imposing a strong taste of its own.

When buying oyster sauce, look for a relatively thin sauce with a light-brown color. If the sauce is dark brown, very thick or has a foamy substance on the top of the jar, it is not of good quality. Unfortunately, F.D.A. food regulations in this country demand that extra salt be added to preserve the oyster sauce that is imported from Hong Kong and China. As a result, most of the oyster sauce you find in American food shops is terribly salty. The best way to use oyster sauce is diluted with a bit of water; it cuts the salt and gives the sauce a thinner, more desirable consistency.

Oyster sauce is frequently used to flavor and thicken other sauces, but its primary use is as a condiment. My favorite way to use oyster sauce is drizzled over steamed or stir-fried vegetables. A simple plate of steamed spinach can be transformed into a rich, exotic dish with just a touch of oyster sauce on top. Use it with Chinese broccoli, mustard greens, *bok choy* (Chinese cabbage) or steamed lettuce. Oyster sauce also makes a good dipping sauce for dumplings, seafood, grilled beef, shish kebab and chicken. It is also a terrific marinade ingredient for steaks, chops and chicken.

BEST BRANDS:
The following brands of oyster sauce are all imported from Hong Kong. Aside from being overly salty, they are all of excellent quality.

Fook Cheong Hing Oyster Sauce
Hop Sing Lung Oyster Sauce Company
Koon Chun Sauce Factory Oyster Sauce
Lee Kum Kee Panda Brand Oyster Sauce

Plum (or Duck) Sauce: Chinese

Plum sauce is that sweet, chutney-like goop that comes in those clear little plastic packets you always find in Chinese restaurants. Nine times out of ten, it's pretty dismal stuff. Most commercially made brands of plum sauce are loaded with sugar (it's usually the main ingredient) and preservatives. There are, however, some brands that are truly good.

TASTING NOTES:
Plum sauce is made from plums, apricots, chile peppers, garlic, vinegar and sugar; sometimes ginger or sweet potatoes are added, too. It is traditionally served with Chinese duck (which is where it gets its nickname from), but it also makes a delicious dipping sauce for chicken, shrimp, spring rolls and steamed or fried dumplings. Plum sauce can also be used as a glaze for roast pork, spareribs, chicken and roast meats.

BEST BRANDS:

Amoy Plum Sauce—Made with plums, sweet potatoes, vinegar, chile peppers and sugar, this sauce makes a wonderful dipping sauce for fried chicken wings.

Dynasty Plum Sauce—This stuff is very sweet and very tasty.

Koon Chun Sauce Factory Plum Sauce—Made in Hong Kong, this is a well-flavored, slightly spicy sauce.

The Silver Palate Plum Chutney—I know they call it a chutney, but to me this is the ultimate plum sauce. Made by a Manhattan specialty food store, this is a sweet, slightly spicy chutney that has an incredibly fresh flavor. Use it as a glaze for roast pork or spareribs or with curries and omelettes.

Satay *Sauce: Indonesian and Chinese*

Satay, or barbecue, is the national dish of Indonesia. Each island prepares its *satay* differently, and for each variation there is a different type of *satay* sauce. The traditional sauce is a rich, thick blend of ground peanuts, tamarind, chiles, garlic, coconut and shrimp paste. (See page 193 for a peanut and chile *satay* sauce recipe.)

TASTING NOTES:

Satay sauce is served with pork, chicken or beef barbecue. It also makes a delicious topping for cold Chinese noodles or a spicy dip for shish kebab, grilled shrimp or raw vegetables.

BEST BRAND:

Kimlan Satay Paste—This is very exotic tasting. It's a combination of soy sauce, peanuts, chile peppers, onion, garlic and shrimp. At first I wasn't thrilled, but this sauce grows on you.

Satay Sauce—Made in Taiwan by Tham-Ky Products, this sauce is fishy and slightly sweet. It's made from coconuts, chile peppers, sesame seeds, dry shrimp, fish, onions and garlic. Serve with barbecue meats and chicken.

Soy Sauces: Chinese and Japanese

Soy sauce is believed to be one of the oldest condiments in the world. The story goes that some 2,500 years ago the Chinese created a fermented fish and meat sauce they called *chiang*. Years later, as Buddhism became increasingly popular, the Chinese substituted soybeans for fish and meat so that they could continue to use the sauce as part of their new vegetarian diet.

Soy sauce made its way to Japan in the early part of the sixth century. The Japanese took an immediate liking to the sauce but found that it overpowered the natural flavors of their food. So they experimented with the basic recipe of soybeans, wheat, salt and water. By adding a higher proportion of wheat and allowing the sauce to ferment over a long period of time, the Japanese created a lighter, more delicate version of soy sauce. By the fifteenth century, soy sauce became so popular in Japan that the Japanese began commercially producing their own type of soy sauce called *shoyu*.

We definitely don't associate soy sauce with European cuisine, but in the seventeenth century Dutch traders exported jugs of the Oriental sauce from Nagasaki to Europe. Initially, it was considered an exotic seasoning that only the elite could afford. King Louis XIV of France was so taken by its flavor that he served it at his most elaborate court banquets.

Soy sauce was first exported to this country in the late eighteenth century when Japanese workers living here became homesick for it. Needless to say, it became very popular with Americans as well.

The first stage in making traditional, naturally brewed soy sauce is called *koji*—a Japanese word meaning "bloom of mold." Essentially, soybeans and wheat are mixed with a starter yeast called Aspergillus. The mixture is placed into large perforated vats where it matures for about three days.

In the second step, a brine or water and salt solution is added, and the mixture is transferred to deep fermentation tanks where it is kept for anywhere from six months to three years. This is the most

crucial stage in making soy sauce. As the mixture ages, the sauce develops its sweet, salty, tart flavor and its rich aroma and deep, dark-brown color.

The final step involves pressing the raw soy sauce from the soy "cake" (which consists of the fermented soybean and wheat hulls). The sauce is then refined and pasteurized before being bottled.

As with most everything else these days, there is also a high-tech, synthetic method for making soy sauce that allows the whole process to occur in about three to four days. Instead of allowing the sauce to age and develop flavor naturally, the soybeans are boiled with hydrochloric acid in order to induce fermentation. Salt is then added along with corn syrup for sweetness and caramel for color. Many of these synthetically produced soy sauces are made in the United States and labeled under Chinese-sounding brand names. They are generally cheaper than naturally brewed soy sauce (although it's really only a matter of a few cents), but they have a definite artificial flavor.

The best way to tell the difference between a bottle of naturally brewed and synthetic soy sauce is to read the label. Look for the words "naturally brewed." This is your guarantee that the traditional, natural process has been used. Next, read the ingredients listed on the label. A really good soy sauce is made only from soybeans, wheat (which is sometimes listed as flour), salt and water. Stay away from brands that contain additives or sweeteners. Another test is to take a bottle of soy sauce and shake it vigorously until bubbles form on the top. If the soy sauce has been naturally fermented, it will form a thick, foamy head, similar to beer, that will take a few seconds to subside.

There are dozens of varieties of soy sauce sold in this country, the majority of which come from China, Hong Kong and Japan. Most people think they all taste pretty much the same, but there is a big difference between light and dark soy and Japanese and Chinese soy sauce. Each sauce has its own distinct flavor, color, aroma and consistency and each one is meant to be used differently. What follows is a brief description of the most common types of soy sauce, along with suggestions for those brands I consider superior and hints on how and when they should be used.

Chinese Soy Sauce

Chinese soy sauce tends to have a stronger, saltier flavor than Japanese soy sauce. Because Chinese soy sauces contains less wheat than the Japanese sauces, they also tend to have a more pronounced soy flavor.

Throughout China it's not uncommon to find dozens of different varieties of soy sauce. In the United States, however, there are essentially three basic types of soy sauce. They are as follows:

Light (or Pale or Thin) Soy Sauce: Light soy sauce is taken from the top of the fermentation tanks while the heavier, darker sauces come from the bottom. This is the most versatile type of Chinese soy sauce. It is used primarily as a table condiment and dipping sauce but can also be used for cooking when you want a light soy flavor.

Black (or Dark or Thick) Soy Sauce: The addition of caramel gives this soy sauce its rich color, thick consistency and sweet flavor. Although it is sometimes served as a table condiment, dark soy sauce is primarily used for cooking, particularly with stir-fried foods.

Use dark soy sauce to add flavor to soups, stews, casseroles and roasts. It's also delicious in marinades for beef, pork, chicken and spareribs.

Heavy (or Double Black) Soy Sauce: This is the least popular variety of Chinese soy sauce, probably because the addition of molasses makes it rather heavy and sweet. It is used, almost exclusively, in cooking and is prized in China for its rich dark color. Use sparingly; heavy soy sauce can easily overpower delicately flavored foods.

TASTING NOTES:
- Sprinkle light Chinese soy sauce over cold tofu with sesame seeds and flakes of dried bonito (fish).
- Light Chinese soy sauce has a slightly sweet flavor that goes particularly well with shrimp. Try stir-frying shrimp, pea pods, peanuts and thinly sliced scallions in a mixture of peanut oil and sesame oil. Add a liberal dash of soy sauce and serve.
- Mix soy sauce with garlic and ginger and serve as a dipping sauce for grilled chicken, *dim sum,* or fried dumplings.
- Try stir-frying snow peas in butter and add a touch of light soy at the last minute. It makes a dark-brown buttery sauce that complements the sweet flavor of the peas.
- Add a dash of soy sauce to vinaigrettes and serve with a green salad.
- Serve black Chinese soy sauce with grilled pork chops and seafood shish kebab.

BEST BRANDS:
China Bowl Light Soy Sauce—According to the label, this delicate sauce is "fermented and aged for at least 120 days." Made in Hong Kong, it is now available in many grocery stores in this country; it makes an ideal table condiment.

Golden Label Soy (Han River Brand)—Made in China, this light soy sauce has a pungent, salty flavor that goes well with a wide variety of foods.

[179]

Joyce Chen's Soy Sauce—Joyce Chen, cookbook author and owner of the Joyce Chen Restaurant in Cambridge, Massachusetts, has created a whole line of Chinese condiments and sauces. The *Light Soy Sauce* is amber-colored, sweet and full of good flavor. It's an ideal table condiment and makes a great base for dipping sauces. Try adding a few drops to salad dressings. Joyce Chen also makes a *Dark Soy Sauce* which has a rich, mahogany color and a pungent, slightly salty flavor. Both sauces are naturally brewed in China.

Pearl River Bridge Soy Superior—Made in China, this is an extremely good, all-purpose dark soy sauce. It's perfect for dipping sauces and is good sprinkled over rice, noodles and soups or with stir-fried vegetables, fish, meat or chicken.

Yuet Heung Yuen Company Soy Sauce—Made in Hong Kong, this is a very reputable brand of traditionally brewed soy sauce.

Wan Ja Shan Soy Sauce—This is a great discovery. Brewed with what seems to be the perfect balance of soybeans, wheat and salt, this traditional light Chinese sauce is delicious. Use it as a table condiment, dipping sauce or with stir-fried foods.

Japanese Soy Sauce (Shoyu)

On the whole, Japanese soy sauces are more delicate, less salty and a bit sweeter than the Chinese variety. After experimenting for hundreds of years, the Japanese discovered that by adding equal quantities of soybeans and wheat, a sweeter soy sauce resulted. Many people believe that the additional wheat also gives the sauce a milder, more well-rounded flavor.

TASTING NOTES:
Japanese soy sauce can be used for cooking or as a table condiment. It's delicious with broiled fish, noodles and steamed vegetables. Add it to stews, soups and casseroles or use as a dipping sauce. Mixed with hot peppers and sesame seeds, it makes a great

dipping sauce for grilled steak or shrimp. Because soy sauce contains enzymes that tenderize foods, it is an especially good ingredient for marinades.

Soy sauce mixed with a touch of *wasabi* (green Japanese horseradish root) is the traditional dipping sauce for *sushi* and *sashimi*. According to Kinjirō Ōmae and Yuzuru Tachibana in *The Book of Sushi*, "Because of the way it masks the rawness of fresh uncooked fish and harmonizes with such other ingredients as seaweed, soy sauce is indispensable to *sushi*. Indeed, it could be said that without soy sauce, *sushi* would probably never have reached its present state of development."

BEST BRANDS:
Chico-San's Lima Soy Sauce—Made in northern Japan and imported by Chico-San of California, this is an exceptionally delicate soy sauce. It's been made by the same family for over ten generations.

Kikkoman Naturally Brewed Soy Sauce—In the last few years, Kikkoman has become America's most popular soy sauce. It's sold in grocery stores and Oriental food stores across the country.

Kikkoman has been around for quite a while. According to the company's brochure: "The art of making soy sauce gradually evolved through the years and by the seventeenth century, the forerunner of modern soy sauce had been created. There were a number of locations in Japan where soy sauce was made. Among them, the city of Noda was the largest and most famous, due to its proximity to the source of raw materials and to the Edo River, the primary means of transporting the finished product to the major market of Edo (today's Tokyo). Around the middle of the seventeenth century, two Noda families, the Mogis and the Takanashis, established breweries and began producing Kikkoman soy sauce."

Today, Kikkoman has offices throughout Asia and the United States. The Kikkoman soy sauce we buy in this country is made at the company's brewery in Walworth, Wisconsin. Although there are now dozens of different brands of Japanese soy sauce sold in this country, Kikkoman remains one of the best all-purpose soy sauces.

Kikkoman Lite Soy Sauce—Dubbed as a "moderately low sodium" sauce, this is brewed in the same manner as regular Kikkoman soy sauce but after fermentation, 43 percent of the salt is extracted. Surprisingly, you hardly notice the difference. (A half teaspoon of Lite Soy Sauce contains 90 milligrams of sodium.) Use as you would regular soy sauce.

Yamasa Soy Sauce—Made in Japan, this soy sauce has a truly refined flavor that goes well with a wide variety of foods.

Tamari: *Japanese-American*

Tamari and soy sauce look, taste and smell almost identical. But, unlike soy sauce, *tamari* has always been sold as a "health food" product "free from preservatives and additives." The truth is *tamari* is practically the same thing as naturally brewed soy sauce. The major difference is that *tamari* contains very little, if any, wheat. (Most soy sauces contain from 30 to 50 percent wheat; *tamari* generally has only 10 percent wheat.) Because there is less wheat, *tamari* tends to have a full (some call it strong) soy flavor.

TASTING NOTES:
Use *tamari* as you would a full-flavor soy sauce. It makes a delicious salad dressing mixed with lemon juice and a light olive (or pure peanut) oil. One of my favorite dishes is fresh bluefish marinated in *tamari*, ginger and garlic and then broiled; see recipe on page 199.

BEST BRANDS:
Eden Tamari Sauce—Made in Japan, this all-natural *tamari* is aged three years before being bottled. It has a rich, slightly salty flavor.

Llama Tamari—Naturally aged for two years in wooden kegs, this *tamari* is a bit salty, but has an incredibly good flavor. It's made in

Brattleboro, Vermont, and goes particularly well with salads.

Mandarin Chef Tamari Sauce—This is an absolutely terrific sauce. Aged for at least 18 months, it has a rich, smooth flavor that is wonderful in soups, stews, vegetable dishes, salads and as a dipping sauce for grilled chicken or barbecued steak.

New England Organic Center Tamari—Aged in wood for three years, this *tamari* has a good flavor and a rich, deep color.

San-J Tamari Natural Soy Sauce—"Naturally brewed and aged for over 4 seasons in wooden casks," this wheat-free sauce is a Japanese favorite. It has a mellow richness that goes well with a wide variety of foods.

Soken-Kimbue Brand Tamari—Aged for over two years, this is a smooth, all-purpose sauce.

Walnut Acres Tamari Soy Sauce—Made at an organic farm in Penns Creek, Pennsylvania, this *tamari* has a good, fresh soy flavor. Walnut Acres also makes a *Wheat-Free Tamari*.

Goma: *Japanese*

This thick, sesame-seed-flavored soy sauce is traditionally served as a condiment with *shabu-shabu*, the Japanese equivalent of beef fondue. It is made from toasted and ground sesame seeds mixed with Japanese soy sauce, *dashi* (a light, Japanese, kelp-flavored broth) and sugar.

TASTING NOTES:
Goma makes a fantastic dipping sauce for grilled chicken, raw vegetables, fish or steak. Mix in a teaspoon of sesame oil and serve it with a cold tofu salad or grilled shrimp.

BEST BRAND:
Meishoku of Japan (distributed by Nishimoto Trading Company) makes a delicious, thick *goma*.

[183]

Ketjap Manis *or* Ketjap Benteng: *Indonesian*

This thick, sweet, almost syrupy Indonesian soy sauce is made with the addition of sugar, molasses and assorted spices. The Indonesian word *"ketjap"* means "a sauce added to food for extra flavor." Some etymologists believe this is the root of our word for "ketchup" or "catsup"; see page 146 for more.

TASTING NOTES:
Ketjap Manis is served with a wide variety of Indonesian dishes and is always present at the traditional Indonesian banquet called *rijsttafel.* It's particularly good served with *satay* (Indonesian barbecue), grilled fish, chicken or steamed vegetables.

BEST BRANDS:
Conimex Ketjap Benteng Manis (Sweet Soy Sauce)—Conimex makes a whole assortment of Indonesian condiments, spices and sauces; this *ketjap* is one of their best products. It's very sweet and spicy—ideal with Chinese-style noodle dishes or added to soups, sauces and gravies.
Conimex Salty Ketjap Benteng Asin—This is a salty version of Indonesian soy sauce. It makes a terrific dipping sauce or marinade ingredient for barbecued meats, chicken or fish.
Go-Tan Ketjap Manis—Made in Kesteren, Holland, this sauce is thick, sweet and full of the delicious flavor of anise. It's an ideal sauce to add to stir-fried vegetables, meats or shrimp. Use it as a dipping sauce for grilled chicken or noodle dishes.

Mushroom Soy Sauce: Chinese

Mushroom soy sauce is a naturally fermented Chinese soy sauce made with the addition of mushrooms. The mushrooms are added toward the end of the fermentation process and they give this sauce a rich, earthy flavor.

TASTING NOTES:
Use mushroom soy sauce for stir-frying vegetables, meats, poultry and fish. Sprinkle it over rice and noodle dishes and into soups and stews. Its flavor can quickly become addictive.

BEST BRANDS:
Pearl River Brand Mushroom Soy—Made in China, this is one of my favorite soy sauces. The mushroom flavor is subtle enough so as not to overpower the sauce, but it does make its presence known. It makes an excellent dipping sauce for vegetables or grilled chicken. It's wonderful over a grilled steak smothered in sautéed mushrooms.

Ponzu *Sauce: Japanese*

This delicious, citrus-flavored soy sauce is a traditional accompaniment to *shabu-shabu*, the Japanese version of fondue. *Ponzu* sauce and *goma* (see page 183) are served side by side with the *shabu-shabu* dish.

Ponzu sauce is a light Japanese soy sauce flavored with rice vinegar, lemon and lime juice. You can make your own simply by mixing ½ cup lemon juice, ½ cup lime juice with 1½ cups Japanese soy sauce and ⅓ cup Japanese rice vinegar. Add *mirin* (a sweet Japanese rice wine) to taste.

TASTING NOTES:
Serve *ponzu* sauce with *shabu-shabu* or over a crisp vegetable salad, grilled fish or chicken. It's wonderful sprinkled over a cold seafood and avocado salad.

BEST BRANDS:
The following brands, all made in Japan, are excellent:

Mitsukan Pon Shabu
Pokka Ponzu Seasoning Soy (Distributed by Daiei Trading Company)
Yamasa Ponzu Soy Sauce

Tentsuyu *Sauce: Japanese*

This flavored soy sauce is a traditional accompaniment to tempura (batter-fried fish and vegetables). There are a number of brands of prepared *tentsuyu* on the market; unfortunately, most of them are filled with M.S.G. and other preservatives. You can make your own simply by heating up ½ cup *dashi* (a light Japanese stock made from kelp and seaweed) or water with 1½ tablespoons light Japanese soy sauce and 1½ tablespoons *mirin* (a sweet Japanese rice wine); add sugar to taste. It's also nice to add a touch of grated ginger to the sauce. Serve warm as a dipping sauce with assorted tempura or with Japanese noodle dishes, grilled chicken or broiled fish.

BEST BRANDS:
Higashimaru and *Kikkoman* both make well-flavored sauces.

Teriyaki *Sauce: Japanese*

Teriyaki literally means "glaze-broil," which refers to a method of cooking meats, fish and poultry that originated in Japan centuries ago. The original *teriyaki* sauce was made simply of soy sauce and *mirin* (sweet Japanese rice wine) with a touch of sugar. It was used primarily to marinate and baste broiled fish.

When the Japanese began emigrating to Hawaii, they altered the sauce by adding local seasonings—fresh ginger, brown sugar and green onions. Most of the commercially produced *teriyaki* sauces sold in the United States today are based on this Hawaiian recipe.

TASTING NOTES:
Although *teriyaki* sauce is still used as a marinade ingredient or as a basting (or glazing) sauce, it also makes an excellent condiment. Sprinkle it over stir-fried vegetables, broiled chicken or fish and salads. It's particularly delicious as a dipping sauce for tempura or fried chicken. It's easy to make your own *teriyaki* sauce; see page 192 for a recipe.

BEST BRANDS:
Kikkoman Teriyaki Barbecue Marinade Sauce—This stuff is terribly sweet on its own but does make a good marinade ingredient for

spareribs, chicken, pork or beef. It's also a good dipping sauce for steamed dumplings, vegetables and barbecued pork.

Wan Ja Shan Teriyaki Sauce—Less sweet than most, this *teriyaki* sauce makes a delicious dipping sauce for shrimp, chicken and beef. It's also nice as a glaze for fish filets such as bluefish, salmon or haddock.

Sweet-and-Sour Sauce: Chinese-American

The contrast of sweet and sour flavors is an ancient Chinese culinary tradition. There are endless variations of sweet-and-sour sauce, all based on the combination of sugar, vinegar and fruit. Unfortunately, most Americans' idea of sweet-and-sour sauce is that pinkish-red, gooey sweet stuff that is glopped onto chicken and fish in almost every Chinese restaurant in America. Capitalizing on America's familiarity with sweet-and-sour sauce, many companies are now marketing a Westernized version of Chinese plum sauce, which they call "sweet-and-sour sauce."

TASTING NOTES:
These sauces can be used for dipping fried shrimp, chicken or fish, or served as a condiment with stir-fried beef, spring rolls and dumplings. Sweet-and-sour sauce makes a delicious glaze for roast ham and spareribs.

BEST BRANDS:
China Bowl Sweet and Sour Ginger Sauce—This looks like it's going to be just another sweet Chinese-style sauce, but it's not—it's fantastic. Thin julienne slices of fresh ginger mixed with hot red chile peppers and scallions float in a thick sauce made of rice vinegar and sugar. Use it as a table condiment for roast pork,

spareribs, spring rolls and *dim sum*, or as a glaze for duck, pork or chicken. China Bowl also makes a delicious, plain *Sweet and Sour Sauce*. It makes a particularly good dip for fried shrimp and dumplings.

Tonkatsu *Sauce: Japanese*

This is a dark, spicy sauce that is traditionally served with *tonkatsu*—Japanese-style fried pork cutlet. Made from tomatoes, apples, carrots and onions, *tonkatsu* sauce is like a thick, spicy Japanese version of ketchup.

TASTING NOTES:
Serve *tonkatsu* sauce with fried pork, chicken or fish. It's also delicious on hamburgers with thinly sliced scallions.

BEST BRANDS:
Several Japanese companies make *tonkatsu* sauce—*Bull Dog, Ikari* and *Kagomé* are all excellent.

MAKING YOUR OWN ORIENTAL SAUCES

Homemade Flavored Soy Sauce

There are an amazing number of flavored soy sauces available in Oriental markets and specialty food stores these days. But a quick look at the list of ingredients reveals that all there is to most of them is soy sauce mixed with one or two flavoring ingredients, lots of sugar and loads of preservatives. What's the point?

Making flavored soy sauce at home is simple and inexpensive. The key is to use your imagination. It's amazing how easily soy sauce mingles with other flavors. *The basic "recipe" for making flavored soy sauce is: ½ cup soy sauce mixed with 2 to 3 tablespoons of flavoring ingredients.* There's usually no need to add sugar or salt; the soy sauce is already sweet and salty.

Homemade flavored soy sauce makes a wonderful gift. Pour the soy sauce out of its bottle and mix with the flavorings. Then, funnel the sauce back into the bottle and place your own label describing the sauce over the one already on the bottle. You can also place a piece of decorative fabric and ribbon over the cap. Be sure to keep these flavored soy sauces refrigerated.

Listed below are a few of my favorite combinations. Use them as dipping sauces with *sushi* and *sashimi,* grilled shrimp, dumplings, Chinese stir-fries and shish kebab. They are also delicious sprinkled over grilled meats, poultry and fish and as a base for salad dressing.

Favorite Flavored-Soy-Sauce Combinations

- Soy sauce mixed with *wasabi* (ground Japanese horseradish)
- Soy sauce with lemon and lime juice and thinly sliced scallions
- Chile-pepper-and-scallion-flavored soy sauce
- Orange-flavored soy sauce (with fresh orange juice and grated orange rind)
- Soy sauce flavored with sesame paste and sesame oil
- Hot Chinese-mustard-flavored soy sauce
- Soy sauce with Japanese rice vinegar, minced fresh ginger and scallions
- Soy sauce with minced pickled plums
- Soy sauce with grated ginger, garlic and sesame oil
- Soy sauce with grated *daikon* (Japanese radish)
- Soy sauce with dry Chinese mustard and red wine vinegar
- Soy sauce with hot chile oil and chopped roasted peanuts

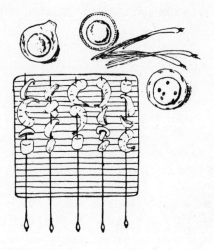

Homemade Teriyaki Sauce

Although there are a few good commercially produced brands of *teriyaki* sauce, most of them are filled with sugar and preservatives. This is a simple, not-too-sweet recipe for making your own. It will keep in the refrigerator for several weeks.

Use as a dipping sauce for raw vegetables and fried foods, or spoon over rice and noodle dishes. The sauce is also delicious as a marinade for meat, chicken or fish, and as a glaze for *teriyaki*.

½ cup plus 2 tablespoons light Japanese soy sauce
½ cup *mirin* (sweet Japanese rice wine)
1½ teaspoons rice vinegar
1½ teaspoons brown sugar
2 teaspoons finely minced fresh ginger
2 cloves minced garlic

In a medium bowl, mix all the ingredients and let sit, covered, for about 2 hours. You can either serve the sauce as is, or strain out the bits of ginger and garlic. Keep refrigerated. *Makes about 1 cup.*

Peanut and Chile Satay Sauce

This thick, spicy *satay* sauce can be served with barbecued pork, chicken or beef. It also makes a delicious dip for raw vegetables, or a topping for cold Chinese noodles.

½ cup chunky peanut butter
3 thinly sliced fresh chile peppers, with seeds
1 large clove minced garlic
1 tablespoon sugar
½ teaspoon cayenne pepper
2½ tablespoons lime juice
2½ tablespoons Chinese dark soy sauce
1½ tablespoons peanut oil
2 tablespoons water

Mix together the peanut butter, chiles, garlic, sugar and cayenne pepper. Stir in the lime juice, soy sauce, oil and water until smooth. Let the *satay* sit at room temperature for 30 minutes before serving. *Makes about ½ cup.*

Ginger-and-Garlic-Flavored Soy Sauce with Radishes

Thinly sliced radishes mixed with soy sauce, rice vinegar, ginger and garlic create this unusual condiment. You can use this as a dipping sauce with fried fish, chicken or tempura. It's also delicious spooned over steamed rice, stir-fried vegetables, salads, grilled fish, or even a steak. Don't make this sauce too far ahead of time because the radishes will lose their crunchy texture after about 24 hours.

20 radishes, very thinly sliced
 1 tablespoon minced fresh ginger
 2 cloves garlic, minced
⅓ cup light soy sauce
⅓ cup rice vinegar
 1 tablespoon sesame oil
 3 tablespoons *mirin* (sweet Japanese rice wine)

Place the radishes in a large bowl and mix in the remaining ingredients. Cover and place in the refrigerator; let marinate 2 to 4 hours and serve cold. *Makes about 1 cup.*

Hot and Spicy Dipping Sauce

This sauce goes well with all sorts of rice and noodle dishes, but it is outrageously good with fried chicken. To make a Chinese-style fried chicken, heat about 4 cups pure Chinese peanut oil in a wok along with a tablespoon of sesame oil and a few slivers of fresh garlic and ginger. Let the oil get very hot. Lightly flour chicken pieces and deep-fry until crisp and completely cooked, about 20 to 25 minutes. Drain on paper towels and serve with this pungent sauce.

        5 tablespoons light Chinese soy sauce
    1½ tablespoons finely minced fresh ginger
        1 teaspoon thinly sliced fresh chile pepper, red or green
        1 tablespoon Oriental sesame oil

Mix all the ingredients in a small saucepan and heat over a moderately low heat for about 5 minutes. Taste for seasoning; if the sauce is too spicy, add additional soy sauce. Serve warm. *Makes about ½ cup.*

Vietnamese Sweet-and-Sour Fish Sauce

Serve this sweet-and-sour dipping sauce with fried noodles, fish or chicken. Covered, it will keep in the refrigerator for several weeks.

 ¼ cup fish sauce, see page 170
 ½ cup cold water
 2 tablespoons fresh lime juice
 2 tablespoons sugar
 ½ teaspoon chopped fresh hot-red chile pepper or 1 small
   dried red pepper, crumbled
 1 clove minced garlic

In a small bowl, whisk together all the ingredients until the sugar is dissolved. Serve at room temperature. *Makes about 1 cup*.

COOKING WITH
ORIENTAL SAUCES

Soy and Tahini Dressing

This dressing is delicious on a salad made of romaine, Boston lettuce and watercress. It's also good on a cold steamed vegetable salad.

  1 teaspoon Dijon mustard
  1 teaspoon sesame tahini
  ⅛ teaspoon freshly grated black pepper
  2½ teaspoons light Chinese or Japanese soy sauce
  1 teaspoon lemon juice
  1½ teaspoons sesame oil
  3 tablespoons red wine vinegar, or rice vinegar
  4 teaspoons olive oil, preferably virgin or extra virgin

In a large salad bowl, stir together the mustard, sesame tahini and pepper to form a smooth paste. Add the remaining ingredients in the order listed and stir until smooth. *Makes about ¼ cup of dressing.*

Stir-Fried Chinese String Beans with Chinese Sausage and Oyster Sauce

This dish takes only a few minutes to cook, so all your ingredients should be pre-chopped and ready to go.

1 tablespoon peanut oil
1 tablespoon sesame oil
2 cloves minced garlic
1 small minced shallot
1 tablespoon minced fresh ginger
2 Chinese pork sausages, thinly sliced
1 pound long Chinese string beans or fresh string beans, cut on the diagonal into 1½-inch-long pieces
2½ tablespoons dark Chinese soy sauce
2 tablespoons water
Oyster sauce

Heat a wok or a large skillet over a high heat until hot, about 2 or 3 minutes. Add the oils and heat until almost to the smoking point. Add the garlic, shallot and ginger and cook about 5 seconds, or until they begin to turn golden brown. Add the sausage and cook about 2 to 4 minutes, or until brown. Remove the sausage and seasonings with a slotted spoon and reserve on a paper towel.

Add the string beans to the hot wok and cook 2 to 3 minutes, or until crisp and slightly brown. Add the sausage and seasonings along with the soy sauce and the water. Let the mixture boil for a minute or until slightly thickened and remove from the heat. Place on a serving dish and drizzle the beans with oyster sauce. *Serves 2 as a main course and 4 as a side dish.*

Broiled Bluefish with Tamari, Ginger and Garlic

This is a delicious and simple way to cook fresh bluefish. The *tamari*, together with the ginger and garlic, creates a dark, rich glaze for the fish filet.

2 pounds bluefish filets
1½ tablespoons minced fresh ginger
2 cloves minced garlic
½ cup *tamari*, Chinese or Japanese soy sauce or *teriyaki* sauce
2 tablespoons butter, cut into small pieces

Preheat the broiler. Lightly oil a baking sheet or broiling pan and place the fish in the center. Insert the ginger and garlic into the fish's flesh and pour the soy sauce over the top. Dot with the butter and place under the broiler for about 10 minutes, or until the fish turns golden brown and flakes when tested with a fork. *Serves 4 to 6.*

Steak Marinated in Sweet Japanese Soy Sauce

You can use this pungent marinade with steak (about 1½ pounds) or double the recipe and use with chicken (about a 3-pound chicken, cut into serving pieces). The meat marinates for about 45 minutes (the soy sauce will help to tenderize the meat); it is then broiled or barbecued and the marinade is boiled and used as a sauce.

    ¾ cup Japanese soy sauce
    ½ cup *mirin* (sweet Japanese rice wine)
    2 tablespoons minced fresh ginger
    2 cloves minced garlic
    1 tablespoon frozen orange juice concentrate
    1 tablespoon homemade Chinese hot chile oil (see recipe
      on page 96), or sesame oil
    1 tablespoon honey
 1½ pounds steak
    1 tablespoon cornstarch (optional)

In a large bowl, whisk together all the ingredients, except the cornstarch. Place the meat or chicken into the mixture and toss to coat thoroughly. Let marinate at room temperature for about 45 minutes to an hour.

Preheat the broiler or barbecue. Remove the meat (or chicken) from the marinade and broil or barbecue the meat until cooked.

Meanwhile, place the marinade in a small saucepan and whisk in the cornstarch, if desired. Bring the marinade to a boil over a high heat, reduce the heat, and let simmer for 2 to 4 minutes, or until slightly thickened.

Spoon a few tablespoons of the sauce over the grilled meat or chicken and serve the remaining sauce on the side. *Make about 1½ cups of marinade.*

Chicken in Mushroom Soy Sauce, Vinegar and Garlic Sauce

This dish is based on *adobong*, the national dish of the Philippines. The chicken is marinated in soy sauce, vinegar and garlic and then gently simmered. The chicken is then broiled, while the marinade is reduced into a thick, rich sweet-and-sour sauce. It's a lot simpler than it sounds and delicious served with white rice and a watercress and orange salad.

1 three-pound chicken, cut into serving pieces
1 cup apple cider vinegar
¾ cup soy sauce, preferably mushroom soy
5 cloves garlic, minced
8 peppercorns
2 bay leaves
1½ tablespoons brown sugar (optional)

Place the chicken in a large casserole or saucepan and cover with the remaining ingredients; toss well to thoroughly coat the chicken pieces. Let marinate at room temperature for a least 1½ hours.

Over a moderately high heat, simmer the chicken until it is tender but not completely cooked, about 15 minutes. Preheat the broiler. Remove the chicken from the sauce and place on a broiling rack. Broil for about 10 minutes, or until the chicken is crisp, brown and cooked (when pierced with a fork or knife, the juices should be yellow and not pink).

Meanwhile, let the sauce boil over a high heat, skimming off any fat that surfaces to the top. Let boil until it is thickened and reduced by half, about 10 minutes. Strain the reduced sauce over the chicken and serve. *Serves 3 to 4.*

7

RELISHES, PICKLES
AND SAVORY JELLIES

LATE SEPTEMBER. The days are still hot and summery; the nights
are just beginning to turn cool, almost cold. The fruit trees and
garden are in all their glory, but the first frost threatens. Out come
the old family recipes, the mason jars and canning lids. The
peaches, tomatoes, corn, onions, squash, peppers, beans and herbs
are picked and an entire day—preferably a rainy one—is put aside
for preserving.

Generation after generation of American cooks have gone
through this ritual. Kitchens fill with the pungent scent of vinegar,
herbs and spices as the last summer produce is sliced, chopped,
diced and mixed into dozens of varieties of relishes, pickles and
savory jellies.

The jars are filled, tightly sealed and then placed in the pantry.
Months later, when most of the country is covered with a foot of
snow, the relishes, pickles and jellies packed inside these jars fill us
with the tastes, smells and memories of summer.

RELISHES

In early American cooking, relishes were one of the favorite ways to preserve surplus fruits and garden vegetables. Everything from onions, peppers, cabbage and corn to cranberries, pears, peaches and apples were used.

The recipes varied from region to region, and kitchen to kitchen, but the essential idea was the same: to chop fresh fruits and vegetables, mix them with a spiced vinegar and let them "pickle" for several months. The appeal of these relishes was that they provided "fresh" food during the winter months and they masked the flavor of meat, which was not always of top quality.

For years the only relishes available in this country were the homemade ones that lined the shelves in every family's pantry or "preserve closet." Cooks took great pride in serving a variety of homemade relishes at special meals and celebrations.

In the late 1800s commercial relishes began to appear. Mr. Henry Heinz bottled a sweet pepper relish and, like his other new product, tomato ketchup, it became a popular way of enlivening the flavor of meats, poultry and fish.

At the time, commercially made relish was considered a great new convenience, but over the years convenience seems to have won out over quality. And so now what passes for relish is nothing more than sugar and corn syrup mixed with overcooked cucumbers and peppers. You know what I mean—the bright green, sweet, gelatinous stuff that's served with hot dogs and hamburgers in restaurants and coffee shops across the country.

Recently some commercially made relishes have appeared on the market that are reminiscent of the homemade variety. In grocery stores and specialty food shops, you can now find a wide assortment of relishes that have the fresh taste and texture of the fruits, vegetables, spices and herbs that went into making them. (See Best Brands for a few of my favorites.)

The very best relishes, however, are still the ones that you make at home. Relish is incredibly easy to make; see pages 218–24 for some delicious recipes.

TASTING NOTES:
- Pepper relish is the classic accompaniment to hot dogs and hamburgers. It also goes well with sausages and barbecued meats.
- Relishes go particularly well with spicy foods; try serving an assortment of fresh relishes with curries or meats, chicken and fish that have been grilled in a spicy pepper sauce.
- Serve a homemade pepper relish as a dipping sauce for grilled shrimp, steamed crab or deep-fried, batter-coated vegetables.
- Add a teaspoon of onion, corn or cranberry relish to a sharp cheddar cheese sandwich.
- Turkey, egg and chicken salad take on a whole new flavor when relish is added. One of my favorite recipes is: 2 cups of thinly sliced chicken or turkey mixed with about ½ cup homemade mayonnaise (see recipe on page 161), a tablespoon of Dijon mustard and a tablespoon of red wine vinegar. Add about 3 tablespoons of Five Pepper Relish (see my recipe on page 218), and add ¼ cup chopped walnuts and raisins. Serve with watercress and toasted pumpernickel bread.
- Spread a tablespoon of piccalilli on a sliced turkey, duck or chicken sandwich.
- Serve a corn, onion or cucumber relish with fried chicken.
- Serve chowchow with lamb curry or roast ham.
- Try a spicy tomato relish on a hamburger or grilled flank steak.
- Add a tablespoon of relish to an avocado and beet salad.

BEST BRANDS:
Callaway Gardens Country Store Corn Relish—Every country store I've ever been to sells corn relish. They're all labeled "Made exclusively for ——— Country Store." I think there must be a huge corn relish factory somewhere that makes millions of bottles of relish each year. Most of it is simply awful; the corn tastes like cardboard and the corn syrup/sugar is so overwhelming you can't

taste any of the other vegetables. But this corn relish, made in Pine Mountain, Georgia, is different. It has a fresh, sweet corn taste and, amazingly, the corn still has a crunchy texture. Made from corn, watermelon, peppers and onions, it's delicious with hamburgers, grilled chops and summer salads.

Conimex Atjar Taugé—Pickled bean sprouts, onions, carrots and peppers make up this refreshing and crunchy Oriental-style relish. Serve with Chinese stir-fries, fried dumplings, grilled fish and meats and salads.

Conimex Atjar Tjampoer—This Indonesian relish is a delicious mixture of thinly sliced cabbage, onions, cucumbers, carrots and leeks, pickled in vinegar, paprika, sugar and spices. It has a great crunchy texture that goes well with Indonesian dishes, grilled meat—even a hot dog.

Conner Farm's Vidalia Onion Relish—Georgia's Vidalia onions are probably the sweetest, most flavorful onions in the world. In this delicious relish, they are mixed with cabbage, peppers and pimentos and blended with vinegar and spices. Serve with meats, sausages, chicken and grilled fish.

Fortnum & Mason Chili Tomato Relish—This English relish has a slightly spicy bite and crunchy texture. Made from tomato paste, gherkin pickles, red peppers, vinegar and spices, it's delicious on cold meats and chicken. Try it on a grilled steak sandwich or a hamburger. You can also serve it, like a cocktail sauce, with cold shrimp or raw oysters and clams on the half shell. Fortnum & Mason also makes a refreshing *Cucumber Relish* that goes well with chicken and on sandwiches.

Hawaiian Plantation's Pineapple-Macadamia Jam—This thick, sweet, crunchy combination of fresh Hawaiian pineapple and macadamia nuts is more like a relish than a jam. Whatever you call it, it's absolutely wonderful. Serve it with curries or mix with Dijon mustard to make a hot pineapple-macadamia glaze for ham or duck.

HP English Mustard Piccalilli Chow-Chow—Two of the favorite early American relishes were piccalilli and chowchow. Just what the difference is between the two I'm not sure. After checking over a dozen cookbooks, I've come to the conclusion that sometime over the years both these vegetable relishes lost their individual identities. A traditional piccalilli is made with green tomatoes, peppers and onions, while a traditional chowchow is a more complex combination of cauliflower, green tomatoes, peppers, beans, celery, cucumbers and onions in a spicy mustard-vinegar sauce. HP, an English company, has come up with a relish they call *Mustard Piccalilli Chow-Chow*. It's a fantastic combination of cauliflower, onions and cucumbers pickled in a thick, spicy mustard sauce. Try it with roasts, curries, cheeses, chicken and barbecued meats.

Howard's Famous New England Piccalilli—Thick and chutney-like, this traditional New England piccalilli is fantastic. It's made in Manchester, New Hampshire, from green tomatoes, red and green peppers, onions and cider vinegar. Its very fresh, sweet-and-sour flavor goes well with sandwiches (particularly cheese), hamburgers, hot dogs, sausages and curries. Try spreading some on buttered toast and topping with tuna or egg salad.

More Please Carrots with Whiskey—A puree of carrots laced with Scotch whiskey, this relish is delicious with curries, burgers, grilled fish, chicken and duck. It's also good on crackers with sweet butter.

Sable & Rosenfeld Cucumber/Mustard Relish—Myra Sable and Carol Rosenfeld are two talented cooks from Toronto. They make a number of delicious condiments and this cucumber relish is one of their best. It's made with small slivers of fresh, crunchy cucumber mixed into a mustardy sauce, and is excellent on grilled hot dogs and sausages.

Sarabeth's Kitchen Cranberry Relish—Sarabeth's Kitchen is a tiny bakery/café located on Amsterdam Avenue in Manhattan. They make a wonderful assortment of marmalades, preserves, fruit butters and relishes. Their cranberry relish is tart and tangy and is excellent served with roast turkey, chicken, duck or roast meats.

Texarkana Hot Stuff—This slightly spicy tomato relish is made by the Hilltop Herb Farm in Cleveland, Texas, for Texarkana, a Manhattan restaurant. It's a delicious blend of fresh tomatoes, onions, peppers, horseradish, garlic and vinegar. Serve with barbecued chicken and ribs, hamburgers or with taco chips and guacamole. It's also wonderful in a lettuce and tomato salad.

PICKLES

When I think of pickles I immediately flash to childhood scenes at our neighborhood deli. I can see the large wooden barrels sitting on the sawdust-strewn floor. Inside those barrels were dill, sour and half-sour pickles floating in a spicy vinegar mixture flavored with mustard seeds, peppercorns and bay leaves. Their intense, pungent scent overwhelmed the deli. At least twice a week, I'd go there and buy two huge, crisp dill pickles, a grilled hot dog with mustard and sauerkraut and a cold cream soda. To me, that was heaven.

You can't buy pickles like that in a jar. Commercially made dill, sour and half-sours can't even come close to the flavor of deli pickles. But, I'm happy to say, you can still find delicious, home-made cucumber pickles at many delis across the country.

I could write an entire book on pickles. They are made in practically every country in the world in endless variations. Here I've dealt with just a few, more unusual pickles that are traditionally served as condiments—wonderful treats like pickled onions and walnuts from England, pickled ginger from Japan, pickled okra from the American South, pickled gherkins from France, and more.

TASTING NOTES:
- Serve a selection of pickles as part of an antipasto salad.
- Chop pickles into chicken, turkey, duck and egg salad.
- Serve pickles with hot dogs, hamburgers and sandwiches.
- Finely chop a few pieces of pickled watermelon rind and serve on a barbecued pork sandwich on a thick roll.
- Pickles go well with cold curry salad, particularly a very hot and spicy chicken or beef curry.
- Pickled black walnuts are the traditional English accompaniment to roast beef, but they also go well with roast lamb, duck and pork.

- Finely chop French *cornichons* and mix into a vinaigrette with a few finely chopped pimentos. Serve as a dipping sauce for grilled shrimp, poached salmon or broiled fish.
- Serve watermelon rind pickle and pickled onions at a picnic with fried chicken and herb biscuits.
- Thinly slice pickled onions and serve on a roast beef sandwich.
- Pickled Oriental radishes (see recipe on page 225) are delicious served with Japanese tempura and Oriental-style rice dishes.

Cornichons

Cornichons are very small pickled gherkin cucumbers. Throughout France—from the most chic Parisian restaurants to small, family-run country bistros—these crisp, tart pickles are the traditional accompaniment to pâtés and cold meat platters.

Cornichons are delicate pickles. They are delicious straight out of the jar, but they can also be served with cheeses, smoked meats and fish, roast chicken, cold poached salmon or fried fish. They add a wonderful crunchy texture and piquant flavor to vinaigrettes, mayonnaise, and tartar sauce (see recipe on page 164).

BEST BRANDS:
There are now a number of very authentic tasting *cornichons* sold in the United States. What follows are a few of my favorites:

Amora Cornichons à l'Ancienne—Made in Dijon, France, these tiny *cornichons* are tart and delicious. They're pickled with pearl onions and mustard seeds.

Balducci's French Country-Style Cornichons—Made in France for Balducci's, a Manhattan specialty food shop, these crisp pickles come in an attractive mason jar.

Cornichons in Vinegar—Made in France by Bernard Lafon (and imported by Dean & Deluca of New York), these crisp, very tart gherkins are pickled with sprigs of fresh tarragon. They are truly superb.

Dessaux Cornichons—Tiny gherkin cucumbers, with even tinier pearl onions and sprigs of fresh tarragon, are pickled in a pungent wine vinegar. Made in Dijon, France, these pickles are excellent with cheeses and pâtés.

Pikarome Cornichons—These French-made pickles are very garlicky and delicious; serve them with a selection of pâtés, a crock of sweet butter and a loaf of French bread.

The Silver Palate's Cornichons—These tart and tangy pickles prove that you don't have to be French to make a good *cornichon*. Made by the Manhattan specialty food shop, fresh grape leaves, pearl onions and tiny gherkins are pickled in a delicious wine vinegar to create this wonderful condiment.

Other Pickles

Some of the very best pickles are the homemade ones sold at local country fairs and community barbecues across the country. Look for them; they are almost always made from old family recipes using the very best local vegetables, fruits and herbs.

Listed below are just a few of my favorite, commercially made pickles. They come closest to the fresh taste of homemade pickles.

Callaway Gardens Country Store Watermelon Pickle—Large chunks of watermelon rind float in this golden-colored sugar and vinegar syrup. These pickles, made in Pine Mountain, Georgia, are deliciously spiced with cinnamon and cloves. Serve with curries, barbecued meats and chicken, fried chicken and fish or mix into a salad.

Conner Farms Pickled Vidalia Onions—For the past few years, food writers have been raving about the glories of Georgia's Vidalia onions. Well, they truly are sweeter and more luscious than your average onion and when they're pickled by Conner Farms, they're the ultimate. Serve with fried chicken, roasts, grilled chops, roast ham, chicken, cold salads, pâtés and cheeses. The very best way to eat them, however, is straight from the jar. But beware. According to the people at Conner Farms, these are "pickles so good that people tasting them for the first time have been known to consume the whole jar without stopping."

Crisp Okra Pickles—These delicious pickles are made by Talko' Texas in San Angelo, Texas. Pickled okra is popular throughout the South, but now that these pickles are being sold across the country their popularity is sure to spread. Serve with seafood, fried chicken and rice dishes.

Hayward's Pickled Onions—Made in England, these small onions are pickled in a delicious malt vinegar. They taste almost as good as homemade (see page 226 for my recipe). Serve with cheeses, cold meats and pâtés.

Liebig's Pickled Walnuts—If you've never tasted a pickled walnut then you're in for a major taste sensation. Pickled walnuts look like large black olives marinating in a sweet, dark vinegar and soy sauce mixture. Their taste is not easy to describe; they're kind of tart and pungent like a pickle but they're also meaty like an olive. (To me they don't taste a thing like walnuts.) They are a British tradition with roast beef, but they also go well with cheese and crackers, pâtés, cold roast chicken and ham. Liebig's walnuts are made in England and they're among the best I've tasted.

The Silver Palate's Pickled Wild Cherries—Wild cherries pickled in vinegar, with cinnamon, cloves and sugar, make this a very unique condiment. Made by The Silver Palate, a specialty food shop in Manhattan, they are delicious with roast duck and goose, pâtés, cheeses, or on top of vanilla, cherry or strawberry ice cream.

Texarkana's Pickled Okra—According to Texarkana, the Manhattan restaurant that packages these crisp, crunchy pickles, "okra was brought to Louisiana by the black Africans during the days of slavery." I'm not wild about fresh okra, but these pickles sure are good. They're great with barbecued meats and poultry and also make a terrific accompaniment to a spicy lamb curry.

SAVORY JELLIES

Although I have been known to spread raspberry jelly on a cheese sandwich and jelly made from tiny, ripe strawberries on roast pork, sweet jellies are generally not served as condiments.

Savory jellies—jellies flavored with a variety of herbs, spices and chile peppers—make delicious accompaniments to roast meats, poultry and fish.

Herbal Jellies

Herbal jellies have been popular in Europe since the Middle Ages. Simmering fresh garden herbs into a homemade apple jelly was considered an art and a great delicacy. For years herbal jellies, other than mint jelly, were difficult to find in this country. Recently, however, a number of English and American companies have started making jellies flavored with rosemary, sage, basil, oregano, summer savory, lemon balm, parsley and rose geranium leaf.

Herbal jellies have a wonderful fresh herb scent and a subtle, yet distinctive herb flavor.

TASTING NOTES:
- Herbal jellies are most frequently served with meats—roast beef, lamb or pork or grilled lamb or pork chops.
- Serve herbal jellies with roast chicken, duck and goose.
- Slice a ripe tomato in half, spread with a tablespoon of herbal jelly on top and broil. Serve with roasts.
- Fill hot muffins and homemade biscuits with herbal jelly.
- Heat herbal jelly and serve as a dipping sauce for a vegetable kebab.

- Add herbal jelly to steamed carrots, peas, beets or green beans.
- Whisk herbal jellies into sauces and gravies.
- Heat herbal jellies and use as a glaze for chicken, duck, lamb, ham or shrimp.
- Spread herbal jellies on buttered toast and top with thin slices of cheddar cheese.
- Make an herbal jelly omelette.
- Spread herbal jellies on top of crepes and pancakes.

BEST BRANDS:

Most of the jellies I tasted were so sweet that I could barely decipher the flavor of the herbs. Listed below are a few brands that have a fresh herb flavor that you can actually taste. (See page 230 for a simple recipe for homemade herb jelly.)

Crabtree & Evelyn's Apple & Rosemary Jelly—This sweet, English-made jelly is brimming with the fresh flavor and fragrance of rosemary. Use it in small quantities with pork, lamb, venison or beef. Crabtree & Evelyn also makes four other varieties of herbal jellies; they are good but for some reason not nearly as flavorful as the rosemary jelly. The *Apple & Sage* jelly goes well with lamb and pork; *Apple & Mint* is particularly good with roast lamb and lamb chops; *Apple & Marjoram* can be served with pork or duck dishes; and *Apple & Thyme* with chicken, duck, pork or lamb.

Elsenham Mint Jelly—"Fresh English mint preserved in a sweet and sour jelly," says the label on this pale mint-green sauce. Although sugar is the main ingredient, this jelly does have a delicious, fresh minty taste. It's made in England and is delicious with lamb, game, chicken or beef.

Rosie's Herb Jellies—"I have had a longtime interest in cooking and learned all about baking and jelly making long ago in northern Maine," writes Rose Fisher of Newfields, New Hampshire. She makes a variety of delicious, sweet, fresh-tasting herb jellies. *Rosie's Dill Jelly* is my favorite; it's wonderful with steamed carrots, beans or cold salmon. The *French Tarragon Jelly* has a distinctive tarragon flavor that goes particularly well with roast chicken and turkey.

There's also a wonderful *Wine Jelly*; it's clear and colorless with a sweet, pronounced white wine flavor. Try it with cold meats and chicken or with grilled fish.

Pepper Jelly

The idea of simmering hot chile peppers into a sweet, spicy jelly probably originated in the American southwest. In the last few years, however, hot pepper jelly has become popular across the country.

Hot pepper jelly is made from hot chile peppers, sweet green or red peppers, sugar, vinegar and pectin. The bright-red or green color of the jelly is not natural; a few drops of artificial coloring are added to most commercially made pepper jellies.

TASTING NOTES:
- The most popular way to serve pepper jelly is on crackers with cream cheese.
- Hot pepper jelly is delicious served on just-baked, steaming-hot cornbread.
- Try it on a peanut butter, grilled cheese or cold lamb sandwich.
- Hot pepper jellies are great on steamed green beans, peas and thinly sliced carrots.
- Try heating the jelly and use it as a dip with dumplings, beef fondue, raw vegetables, fried chicken or grilled shrimp.
- Mix a few tablespoons of hot pepper jelly with either sour cream or yogurt and serve as a dip with raw vegetables or taco chips.
- Try pepper jelly (instead of mustard) with a variety of grilled sausages.
- Instead of a traditional pepper relish, serve a hot dog with pepper jelly and sautéed onions.
- Mix pepper jellies into salad dressings.
- Serve pepper jellies with pâtés, cheeses and cold meats.
- Serve pepper jelly, like a mint sauce, with roasts.

BEST BRANDS:

I was amazed to see how many pepper jellies there are on the market. Most of them taste pretty much the same, but the following brands are particularly good.

Bailey's Hot Pepper Jelly—"I've been making pepper jelly for 18 years," writes "Aunt Freddie" Bailey of Natchez, Mississippi. "I am 79 years young. I live in a big, 4-story house. On the first floor of the house is my children's and ladies' boutique and antiques. My jelly kitchen is in the yard. I never get tired of making it." And, Aunt Freddie, I never tire of eating your delicious spicy-sweet pepper jelly. Aunt Freddie suggests serving the jelly with crackers and cream cheese, cheeses, meats and poultry. You can buy Bailey's pepper jellies in red or green, which of course are the colors of Christmas, but according to Aunt Freddie, "It's a nice gift for any season or occasion, because it's just plain good."

Callaway Gardens Country Store Pepper Jelly—These bright-red and green jellies aren't very spicy, but they're delicious with cream cheese and crackers. Made in Pine Mountain, Georgia, they're made from hot chile peppers, sweet red and green peppers, sugar, vinegar and pectin.

Casa Peña Blanca Green Jalapeño Jelly—Casa Peña Blanca, of El Paso, Texas, makes one of the best pepper jellies around. It's a rich, sweet, thick jelly made from the hot, spicy flavor of jalapeño peppers. The addition of Mexican lime juice makes this jelly particularly delicious.

Hawaiian Plantations Hot Pepper Jelly—Made in Honolulu, this hot pepper jelly has a great, spicy bite. Hawaiian Plantations also makes a good *Mild Pepper Jelly* for people who like a pepper flavor without the punch.

Judyth's Mountain Hot Pepper Jelly—Judyth's Mountain of Los Gatos, California, makes two types of pepper jelly: the *Hot Pepper Jelly* is made from equal quantities of sweet peppers and hot chile peppers and the *Hotter Hot Pepper Jelly* is, obviously, heavier on the chile peppers. They both have a sweet flavor and a dark, butterscotch color that's obtained without using any artificial colorings.

My Grandmother's Hot Pepper Jelly—This is an excellent jelly. (I think it might just be my favorite.) Made by Pat Kincaid of Deerfield, Florida, it is very spicy. Start with just a small bit; it has a "bite" that can really creep up on you.

Old San Antonio Jalepeño Jelly—Made in San Antonio, Texas, this spicy jelly is wonderful with taco chips and Tex-Mex food.

Rosie's Red Pepper Jelly—This red-colored jelly, made in Newfields, New Hampshire, is full of good, fresh pepper flavor.

Williamsburg Pepper Jelly—A few years ago, Laurie Lynch of Rye, New Hampshire, decided to market an old family recipe. Her great-great-grandfather, who lived in Williamsburg, Virginia, was famous for his pepper jelly. Lynch has taken this recipe (which uses three types of fresh peppers and not a trace of salt) and bottled it in an old-fashioned-type jar. It's delicious on grilled hot dogs.

MAKING YOUR OWN RELISHES, PICKLES AND SAVORY JELLIES

Boiling Water Bath for Canning Chutneys, Relishes and Pickles

For years I believed that canning was a time-consuming and tedious process. Then, one August afternoon, I tried to can some leftover garden tomatoes and was amazed to see how easy it is. Canning is a perfect and rewarding way to spend a rainy summer afternoon.

Keep in mind that this method is only good for canning foods with a high acid content; all the recipes in this book work with this method. If you have further questions about canning, I recommend *The Joy of Cooking* or the *Ball Blue Book,* published by the Ball Corporation of Muncie, Indiana.

1. Wash jars and lids in hot, soapy water. Sterilize jars and lids in boiling water for 15 minutes. Remove with tongs and invert on a clean dish towel or on paper towels to dry.
2. Fill a water-bath canner with water, or a pot large enough for the jars to be completely immersed and fully surrounded by boiling water. Make sure the pot has a rack on the bottom so the jars won't touch the bottom. (If you don't have a rack, simply wrap the jars in clean tea or dish towels. The jars should not touch each other while being processed.) Bring the water to a rolling boil.
3. Fill the sterilized jars with hot chutney, relish or pickles, making sure to leave at least 1-inch head space.
4. Before placing lids on jars, remove any air pockets in the food using a wooden spoon; *never use metal utensils.*
5. Screw lids tightly on jars and place jars in boiling water. Begin timing when water returns to a boil and process for time called for in recipe.
6. Remove jars with tongs and let cool overnight.
7. To make sure that the vacuum has formed, tap the lids lightly with a metal spoon. If you hear a ringing sound, the jar is safely sealed. But if the sound is dull and hollow, you need to reprocess or simply use the condiment right away. Always store jars in a cool, dark spot.

Five Pepper Relish

The combination of sweet red and green peppers, Italian frying peppers, red chile peppers and black peppercorns makes this a colorful, sweet and slightly spicy relish. It's delicious served with curries, hamburgers, hot dogs, barbecued chicken or as a dipping sauce for shrimp and raw vegetables. Plan on letting the relish sit for about two weeks before serving.

4 medium-sweet red peppers, finely chopped without seeds, about 1½ cups
4 medium-sweet green peppers, finely chopped without seeds, about 1½ cups
8 Italian frying peppers, sliced into thin rings without seeds, about 2 cups
1 small fresh red chile pepper, finely chopped with seeds, about 1½ tablespoons
2 medium onions, finely chopped, about 1½ cups
1 cup granulated sugar
¾ cup cider vinegar
1 tablespoon yellow mustard seeds
½ tablespoon black peppercorns

Mix all the ingredients in a large stainless-steel saucepan and bring to a boil over a high heat. Reduce the heat and simmer, uncovered, for 6 to 7 minutes or until the peppers are just tender but still a bit crunchy.

Place the relish into sterilized mason jars, distributing the liquid evenly, and seal the lid tightly. Process in a boiling water bath for 20 minutes (see pages 216–17 for additional notes on canning), or let cool and refrigerate for two weeks before serving. *Makes about 4 cups.*

Pear Relish in Raspberry Vinegar

Serve this thick, fruity relish with roast chicken, duck, beef or pork. It's delicious on cottage cheese, hamburgers and on a chicken or turkey sandwich. Try it with a warm duck salad with slivers of pears and almonds in a raspberry vinegar and olive oil dressing.

This relish makes a great Christmas gift. Make it in the fall when there's a large variety of fresh pears to choose from.

> 2 large, slightly ripe pears, peeled, cored and coarsely chopped, about 2 cups
> 1 large or 2 small sweet red peppers, chopped, about 1 cup
> 1 medium onion, finely chopped, about 1 cup
> ¾ cup raspberry vinegar
> ½ cup plus 1 tablespoon sugar
> ¼ cup apple cider vinegar
> 1 tablespoon yellow mustard seeds
> 4 peppercorns
> 2 small dried red chile peppers
> ½ teaspoon ground ginger
> ½ teaspoon salt

Mix all the ingredients in a medium-size stainless-steel saucepan. Bring the mixture to a boil over high heat. Reduce the heat and simmer, uncovered, until the relish thickens, about 45 minutes to an hour. Stir the relish frequently to keep it from sticking.

Ladle the hot relish into sterilized mason jars and seal tightly. Process in a boiling water bath for 15 minutes (see pages 216–17 for additional notes on canning), or let cool and refrigerate for two weeks before serving.

Cauliflower-Mustard Pickles

This spicy relish is a simplified version of chowchow—an early American favorite. Serve with cold meats, roast chicken, spicy curries, cheese and with antipasto.

    1 large cauliflower, broken into small florets, about 6 cups
 4½ cups cider vinegar
    2 tablespoons yellow mustard seeds
  ½ tablespoon celery seeds
  ½ tablespoon coriander seeds
  ¼ cup sugar
  ⅓ cup flour
 1½ tablespoons mustard powder
 1½ teaspoons ground turmeric
    1 medium onion, thinly sliced

Place the cauliflower florets in a pot of boiling salted water and boil until slightly tender, about 4 or 5 minutes. (You want the cauliflower to be *almost* cooked, but not falling apart.) Drain and refresh under cold running water and reserve.

In a large stainless-steel pot, mix 3½ cups of the vinegar, the mustard seeds, celery seeds, coriander seeds and sugar. Bring to a boil over moderately high heat.

Meanwhile, in a medium-size bowl, mix the flour, mustard powder, turmeric and the remaining cup of vinegar to form a smooth paste. Once the vinegar mixture comes to a boil, whisk in the paste, a few tablespoons at a time. Let the vinegar mixture boil for 2 to 3 minutes.

Place the cauliflower and onion slices into sterilized pint-size mason jars. Pour the hot vinegar mixture over the vegetables and seal tightly.

Process in a boiling water bath for 20 minutes (see pages 216–17 for additional notes on canning), or let cool and refrigerate for at least two weeks before serving. *Makes 4 pints.*

Spicy Cucumber and Pepper Relish

This relish is based on a Tunisian recipe called *Pfepfel bar Labid* (cucumber and pepper relish). I've added hot chile peppers to give it a spicy bite.

Serve this fresh, simple relish with grilled fish and shellfish, *paella*, curries and salads. Its tart flavor and crunchy texture also complement barbecued meats and chicken.

    2 tablespoons fresh lime juice
    1 teaspoon salt
    1 medium-size cucumber
    1 medium-size green pepper, deseeded and chopped into
       1-inch cubes
    1 tablespoon thinly sliced hot green chile pepper

In a serving bowl, mix the lime juice and salt and set aside.

Peel the cucumber and slice in half lengthwise. Using the back of a spoon, scoop out the seeds and then slice the cucumber into ½-inch-wide pieces. Add the cucumber slices and the peppers to the lime juice and salt and stir to coat evenly. Cover and let marinate for about 6 hours before serving. The relish will keep, refrigerated, for about a day or two—after that time it loses its crunchy texture. *Makes about 2 cups.*

Beet, Horseradish and Apple Relish

This sharp, slightly spicy relish has a beautiful beet-red color. Serve it with roast chicken, pork, lamb or grilled pork chops. It's also good mixed with sour cream and served with ham, roast beef, beef fondue and grilled fish.

    1 large tart red apple, peeled and diced, about ¾ cup
    3 -inch piece fresh horseradish root, peeled and sliced into
       thin strips about 1-inch long, about ⅓ cup
    2 small chopped pickled or cooked beets, with 3
       tablespoons of beet juice (see page 227 for recipe for
       homemade pickled beets)
    2 tablespoons apple cider vinegar

In a small bowl, mix all the ingredients. Cover and refrigerate for at least 4 hours. Serve within 48 hours. *Makes about 1 cup.*

Cranberry, Ginger and Grapefruit Relish

This sweet, tart relish is the perfect condiment to serve with roast turkey, duck, goose, chicken or ham.

    4 cups whole cranberries (1 pound)
 1¼ cups sugar
    ½ cup chopped candied ginger in syrup
    2 tablespoons syrup from the candied ginger
    ¼ cup grapefruit juice
       Grated rind from 1 grapefruit
    ½ cup slivered almonds

In a large saucepan, mix the cranberries, sugar, ginger, syrup, grapefruit juice and rind. Cover and bring to a boil over high heat. Lower the heat and simmer for 10 to 15 minutes, or until the cranberries pop open. Remove from the heat and stir in the almonds. Let cool and place into sterilized jars. Cover with paraffin and keep in a dark, cool place. *Makes about 3 cups.*

Onion and Cassis Relish

Onions and cassis (black-currant liqueur) are a wonderful combination. Serve this savory relish with hamburgers, pâtés, on buttered toast, with pan-fried fish, and with roast chicken or duck.

2 medium-size onions, thinly sliced, about 1½ cups
¾ cup crème de cassis
¼ cup water
¼ cup brown sugar
2 tablespoons red wine vinegar
4 peppercorns
4 cloves
¼ cup golden raisins

Mix all the ingredients, except the raisins, in a stainless-steel saucepan and bring to a boil over a high heat. Reduce the heat and simmer for about 30 minutes, stirring occasionally. Mix in the raisins, let cool, and then refrigerate. The relish will keep for about a week. *Makes 1 cup.*

Tomato-Apple Relish

Connie Weeks lives on a farm in Eliot, Maine. There she makes relishes, chutneys, jellies, jam, honey, spins her own wool and makes her own soap. This simple, delicious recipe is one of her best. "Every gardener has experienced a glut of tomatoes at the end of the gardening season," she writes in her book, *Using Summer's Bounty—A Country Woman's Source Book.* "Last year I had not only too many tomatoes, but also many imperfect apples. In scanning recipes for a solution, I came across the following recipe . . . it makes a sweet relish, an excellent side dish, a fine accompaniment to hamburgers and an interesting addition to a winter salad when fresh vegetables are imported, expensive and often boring."

8 cups peeled, coarsely chopped tomatoes
2 cups diced tart apples
1 cup chopped onion
1 cup chopped celery
2 sweet green peppers, cored and chopped
2 sweet red peppers, cored and chopped
1½ cups cider vinegar
2¾ cups sugar
1 tablespoon yellow mustard seeds
½ tablespoon whole cloves
1 tablespoon ground cinnamon

Place all the ingredients into a large stainless-steel saucepan and cook over a moderate heat for about 2 hours, or until thickened. (Stir the relish occasionally to keep it from sticking to the pan.) Ladle the hot relish into sterilized jars and seal tightly. Process in a boiling water bath for 15 minutes (see pages 216–17 for additional notes on canning), or let cool and place in the refrigerator for a week before serving. *Makes about 3 pints.*

Jessica's Pickled Oriental Radishes

Pickled radishes are an old Japanese tradition. *Daikon*, a large white Japanese radish, is pickled in a sweet soy mixture and then served with grilled fish.

This is an adaptation of that recipe using regular red radishes. It comes from a designer friend, Jessica Weber, of New York, New York.

  1 tablespoon sugar
  5 tablespoons Japanese soy sauce
1½ tablespoons Oriental sesame oil
2½ tablespoons distilled white vinegar, or Japanese rice wine vinegar
 ¼ teaspoon hot pepper sauce
30 radishes, washed and trimmed

In a medium-size bowl, mix the sugar and soy sauce. Whisk in the oil, vinegar and hot pepper sauce. Score each end of the radishes with an X about ⅛ inch deep and toss with the marinade. Cover and, tossing occasionally, refrigerate at least 5 hours and as long as 24 hours. *Makes about 3 cups.*

Pickled Onions

This recipe makes very authentic-tasting English-style pickled onions. Serve them with cheeses, cold meat platters and pâtés.

    2 pounds small white onions (about 32)
       Salt
    2 cups malt or cider vinegar
    1 teaspoon salt
   10 cloves
    8 black peppercorns
    2 bay leaves

Place the onions in a large bowl and cover with boiling water. Let sit for about 4 minutes and then drain. Rinse under cold running water and then carefully peel.

Place the peeled onions in a large, shallow tray or roasting tin and sprinkle liberally with salt. Let sit overnight. The following day, rinse the onions well and dry thoroughly.

In a large stainless-steel pan, heat the vinegar, 1 teaspoon of salt, cloves, peppercorns and bay leaves. Bring the vinegar to a boil over moderately high heat and let boil for 5 minutes. Add the onions and bring the vinegar back to a boil. Remove the onions with a slotted spoon and tightly pack into sterilized pint-size mason jars. Pour the hot vinegar over the onions and seal tightly.

Process in a boiling water bath for 30 minutes (see pages 216–17 for additional notes on canning), or let cool and place in the refrigerator for at least two weeks before serving. *Makes 3 pints.*

J.K.R.'s Pickled Beets

These pickles are wonderful. Fresh beets and onions are simmered and then pickled in an apple cider vinegar and balsamic vinegar mixture. Serve them with cold meats, cheeses, an antipasto platter or eat them on their own.

24 medium beets
8 small onions, peeled
2½ cups apple cider vinegar
½ cup balsamic, sherry or red wine vinegar
2 to 4 teaspoons sugar (optional)

Clean the beets under cold running water. Place the beets in a large pot and cover with water. Boil until *almost* tender when tested with a fork; this will take anywhere from 15 to 35 minutes depending on the size and freshness of the beets. Remove the beets with a slotted spoon (reserving the beet water), peel and cut in half.

Boil the beet water; add the onions and let boil for 2 minutes. Remove the onions with a slotted spoon (again reserving the water), and cut the onions in half.

In a large stainless-steel pot, heat 1 cup of the reserved beet water with the apple cider vinegar and balsamic vinegar; add sugar if you want the beets to be sweet.

Divide the beets and onions equally and place into sterilized, pint-size mason jars. Ladle the hot vinegar mixture over the beets and onions and seal tightly.

Process in a boiling water bath for 30 minutes (see pages 216–17 for additional notes on canning), or let cool and place in the refrigerator for at least two weeks before serving. *Makes 4 pints.*

Gari: *Japanese Pickled Ginger*

Gari, pickled fresh ginger, is traditionally served in Japan with *sushi* and *sashimi*. It is said to freshen your breath and cleanse your palate between pieces of raw fish.

Serve about a tablespoon or two of *gari* per person with *sushi* and *sashimi*. It's also delicious served with other Japanese dishes, barbecued meats and chicken, and seafood shish kebab.

½ pound fresh ginger
1½ tablespoons salt
1 cup Japanese rice vinegar
½ cup water
2½ tablespoons sugar

Peel the ginger with a small sharp knife or peeler. Place on a small plate and sprinkle with the salt. Let sit overnight.

Rinse the ginger to remove the salt and let dry. In a medium-size bowl, mix the vinegar, water and sugar. Add the ginger, cover, and place in the refrigerator or in a cool, dark spot for one to three weeks. The ginger is ready when it turns a subtle pink color. Slice off a thin piece to see if it's pink throughout.

Remove the ginger from the marinade and place in a small bowl. Cover and refrigerate until ready to serve.

To serve *gari*, use either a sharp knife or a food processor and cut the ginger into paper-thin slices *along* the grain. *Makes ½ pound.*

Connie Weeks' Watermelon Rind Pickle

"My family and I have always been fond of this pickle," writes Connie Weeks, a cook from Eliot, Maine. "I have never bought a melon just for making the pickle. I always use the rind from our 4th of July, Labor Day and other summertime celebration picnics." Serve with salads, cold meats, cheese and barbecued chicken.

2 cups watermelon rind pieces, cut into 1-inch-wide slices (be sure to cut all the dark-green skin and the red fruit off the pieces of rind)
¼ cup salt mixed with 4 cups water
2 cups water
2 cups cider vinegar
4 cups sugar
4 cinnamon sticks
2 tablespoons whole cloves

Place the watermelon rind in a large bowl and cover with the salt water. Place a plate over the bowl and weigh it down with a rock or pie weights in order to keep the rind submerged in the water. Let soak in the refrigerator for 12 hours.

Drain the rind and rinse under cold running water. Place the rind in a large pot of boiling water and boil until almost tender when tested with a fork, about 10 minutes. Drain the rind and reserve.

In a large stainless-steel pot, mix the water, vinegar, sugar, cinnamon sticks and cloves. Boil over high heat for 5 minutes. Add the rind and boil about 15 to 20 minutes, or until the rind is clear. (Be careful not to overcook the rind. Stop cooking as soon as the rind is clear, or it will be mushy.)

Remove the rind with a slotted spoon and fill sterilized pint-size mason jars. Pour the hot vinegar mixture and the spices over the rind and seal tightly. Process in a boiling water bath for 15 minutes (see pages 216–17 for additional notes on canning), or let cool and place in the refrigerator for at least two weeks before serving. *Makes about 3 pints.*

Kate Slate's Apple Cider Jelly

This is one of those recipes that's too easy to be true. By simply boiling down a gallon of apple cider, you're left with a naturally sweet, syrupy jelly. Absolutely nothing else is added; the natural sugars and pectin in the apples do all the work. Serve with roast pork or lamb, on top of toast, muffins or ice cream, or with pancakes and waffles.

1 gallon unsweetened apple cider with no additives

In a large, heavy pot, bring the cider to a boil over high heat. Reduce the heat to moderate and cook the cider at a low, rolling boil until it is reduced to 2 cups, about 2 hours. (Toward the end of the cooking time be sure to watch the jelly. You don't want it to get too thick or it will caramelize. You simply want it to thicken to a jellylike consistency.)

Pour the hot jelly into a sterilized canning or jelly jar, close the lid and let cool to room temperature. Refrigerate overnight before serving. The jelly will keep, refrigerated, for several months. *Makes 2 cups.*

Herb-Flavored Jellies

Making an herb-flavored jelly can be simple if you follow the recipe above for apple cider jelly. Wrap about 1 cup fresh herbs (rosemary, basil, thyme, sage, marjoram, parsley or a combination) in a double layer of cheesecloth and place in the pot with the cider. Boil the cider until reduced to 2 cups, pressing down on the cheesecloth every now and then to extract the herb flavor. Place a sprig of fresh herb into a sterilized jelly jar and strain the apple cider jelly on top, discarding the cheesecloth. *Makes 2 cups.*

Apple Cider Jelly with Rose Geranium Leaves

Follow the recipe for apple cider jelly on page 230. Place a clean rose geranium leaf into a sterilized canning or jelly jar and cover with the hot jelly. The leaf will give the jelly a delicate, but distinctive flavor. *Makes 2 cups.*

Hot Pepper Apple Cider Jelly

Follow the recipe for apple cider jelly on page 230. Wrap 4 chopped small chile peppers in a double layer of cheesecloth and place in the pan with the cider. Boil the cider until reduced to 2 cups, pressing down on the cheesecloth every now and then to extract the pepper flavor. Strain the jelly into a sterilized jar and discard the peppers. (The same method can be used to make Apple Cider and Ginger Jelly using a peeled, 2-inch piece of fresh ginger.) *Makes 2 cups.*

Red Currant and Mint Jelly

Serve this simple jelly with meats, game and poultry.

 1 cup red-currant or black-currant jelly
 2 tablespoons chopped fresh mint

Mix the jelly and mint in a small saucepan and place over a moderate heat for 2 to 3 minutes, or until warm and thin. Serve warm or place in the refrigerator, let thicken and serve cold. *Makes 1 cup.*

CHUTNEY

A FRIEND OF MINE recently visited India for the first time and decided to have dinner at one of Bombay's better restaurants. While enjoying a delicious, spicy lamb curry, she innocently asked the waiter to bring a bottle of Major Grey's. He gave her a strange look and curtly said, "Madame, you'd like some Major who?"

What my friend didn't realize is that commercially made chutneys are frowned upon in India. Although you can find bottled chutneys in some Indian food stores (none of which, by the way, go under the name "Major Grey's"), almost all Indian chefs and home cooks take great pride in preparing their own special chutneys. After my friend explained to the waiter what she wanted, he arrived at her table with a huge silver tray filled with a dozen little bowls of freshly made chutneys.

"Chutneys," writes Santha Rama Rau in the Time-Life book *The Cooking of India*, "occupy a position of such importance in the food of almost any part of India, and offer such an astonishing diversity of flavors, such a limitless list of ingredients, that a whole book could be written about their uses, possibilities and significance."

Indian chutneys range from an exotic mixture of grated coconut, tamarind and chile peppers to fresh mint ground with coriander leaves and lime juice. Their flavor can be hot and spicy or slightly sweet, cool and refreshing. What all chutneys have in common is their ability to wake up the flavors in food and provide contrast in taste and texture to the other foods they are served with.

Most of the chutney that makes its way to American food shops comes via England. The British passion for chutney goes back several hundred years. During the eighteenth century, British civil servants and army officers stationed in India brought bottles of chutney back home with them. The British adored these spicy, exotic concoctions and before long chutney was in great demand. British companies began importing chutney in bulk and sold it under labels like Major Grey's, Colonel Skinner and Bengal Club—all names that recalled the days of the British *raj*.

The popularity of chutney in the United States is more recent, but equally passionate. Major Grey's (which is actually a generic name for a sweet-and-spicy mango chutney) has practically become a household word. It seems that even people who won't have anything to do with Indian food know and love this sweet-and-spicy condiment.

⚜

CHUTNEY SURVEY

The word "chutney" is based on the Hindi word *"chatni,"* meaning to lick or taste. *The Oxford English Dictionary* defines it as a "strong relish or condiment compounded of ripe fruits, acids, or sour herbs, and flavored with chillies, spices, etc.," but this simple definition can't capture the many textures and styles of chutney.

Chutneys sold in this country come from England, India, France and all over the United States; they're made with everything from mangoes and bananas to apples and cucumber. Most of them, I'm sorry to say, are absolutely awful. They are so loaded with sugar and sweeteners that you can barely taste the flavors of all the fruits and spices that went into making them. (It's strange, because it's really so easy to make a good, flavorful chutney; see recipes on pages 239–44.) There are, however, a number of commercially made brands that are delicious. See Best Brands.

TASTING NOTES:
Everyone serves chutneys with curries, but there are many other foods that they can complement. Here are just a few ideas:

- Serve a peach chutney on a baked sweet potato or a mango chutney with boiled new potatoes.
- Roast lamb, pork, duck, turkey and chicken are naturals with chutney—either served as a condiment or brushed onto the meat while it's still roasting.
- Chutneys go well with cold meats, cheeses and crackers.
- Garnish a thick, homemade vegetable stew with a spoonful of peach or a spicy pepper chutney.
- Mix chutneys into sauces and mayonnaise.
- Use chutneys to stuff a tenderloin of pork or butterflied lamb or a boneless chicken breast.
- Add a spicy chutney to a cup of yogurt to make a dip for raw vegetables and crisp-fried Indian breads.
- Serve a fresh, spicy coriander chutney on broiled tomato halves or grilled swordfish or salmon.
- Apple, pear and peach chutneys are delicious served with apple and pumpkin pie.
- Sweet mango chutney makes a fantastic topping for a hot fruit compote.
- One of my favorite sandwiches is thinly sliced brown bread, with thin slices of sharp cheddar cheese and mango chutney.
- Spread chutney on thin pancakes or inside pita bread and top with thinly sliced barbecued lamb or grilled steak.
- Chop a few tablespoons of mango chutney and add to deviled eggs.
- Make an apple, peach, pear or mango chutney omelette.

[235]

BEST BRANDS:

Casa Peña Blanca Hot Apple Chutney—Go very easy on this stuff. Made in El Paso, Texas, this is a very thick and spicy chutney. Made with apples, raisins, onions, lots of chile peppers, curry, mustard and other spices, it is outrageously good with roast pork, broiled chicken, in a turkey or duck salad and as a dip for taco chips. Try a sandwich made of black bread, thin slices of ham and a dab of this apple chutney; it's fantastic.

Conimex Star Brand Mango Chutney—This traditional-style mango chutney is filled with slivers of fresh ginger. It has a nice, smooth texture that goes well with curries, meats and poultry.

Cuisine Perel Grape Peach Chutney—Made in Tiburon, California, this chutney combines the best of California fruit and California wine grapes. The peaches in this chutney taste so fresh you can't believe they weren't picked yesterday. Try it in sauces, rice dishes, with roasts and curries and mixed with cream cheese to make a spicy dip. Cuisine Perel also makes a piquant *Grape Apricot Chutney* and a delicious *Grape Pear Chutney*.

Crabtree & Evelyn Chutneys—This London-based company makes five delicious styles of chutneys. Their *Apple Chutney* has a sweet-and-spicy flavor that is excellent with pork chops and roasted sweet potatoes. *Apricot Chutney* is a sweet combination of fresh apricots, raisins, apples and onions. It has a great texture (with chunks of apricot and whole raisins) that goes well with pork, chicken and curries. The *Gooseberry Chutney* is very tart and vinegary. Try it with cheeses, chicken or curries. Prune lovers will really go for their thick (almost pasty) *Prune Chutney*. It's good with all sorts of curries, particularly beef. Tomatoes, apples, onions and raisins go into making a delicious *Tomato Chutney*. "Cooked slowly in open kettles and filled by hand," it's superb on hamburgers, in pasta sauces and in a homemade cream of tomato soup.

Elsenham Chutneys—This reputable Essex, England, company produces four different chutneys. The *Indian Fruit Chutney* is distinctive. Made from a blend of mangoes, papaya, pumpkin, cherries, apples, ginger, raisins, melon seeds, cashews, almonds and pistachios, it is superb with barbecued meats and curries. The *Sweet*

Mango Chutney is not nearly as unique, but it does have a sweet, subtle blend of flavors. *Hot Mango Chutney* is deliciously spicy and the *Indian Tirhoot Chutney* is made from an original Indian recipe using lemon and orange peel, mangoes, tamarind and vinegar.

Lifespice Sweet Heat Chutney—Lifespice was created in New York by Ruth and Hilary Baum "to meet the challenge of pleasing food lovers who are on salt-free or low-salt diets." This extraordinarily good chutney is a spicy blend of apricots, raisins, tomatoes, onions, honey and spices. It's made without a trace of salt and, amazingly, you won't miss the salt in the least. Serve with curries, roasts, in chicken salad and on burgers.

Original Sun Brand Indian Mango Major Grey's Chutney—This is an old favorite of mine. If you're buying a mango chutney, this award-winning brand is one of the best you'll find. From Princess Dock, Bombay, it's a perfect balance of sweet-and-sour flavors nicely spiked with chile peppers, garlic and ginger. The packaging is as distinctive as the chutney itself; look for the bright red-and-yellow sun on the label and the glass jar wrapped in plastic.

Sable and Rosenfeld's Chutney Relishes—Two talented Canadian women created these chutneys; they are both exceptionally good. The *Chopped Fruit Chutney Relish* is thick and spicy and delicious served with steaks, hamburgers, grilled chicken and vegetable curries. The *Chopped Tomato Chutney Relish* is a thick, slightly spicy mixture of tomatoes, peaches, onions and raisins. It can be added to soups, stews and sauces or served with roasts, curries and burgers.

Sinha Trading Co.'s Mango Chutney—The Foods of India, on Lexington Avenue in New York, is a terrific shop filled with all sorts of imported Indian foods. This sweet-and-sour mango chutney is made in India just for them. It is slightly sweet and very fresh tasting. Delicious with *tandoori* chicken, lamb curry and Indian breads.

Subahdar Chutneys—There are four chutneys made under the Subahdar label; they are all made in India and are of very good quality. The *Bengal Club Chutney* is a medium-hot chutney that is thick and delicious. *Hot Sliced Mango Chutney* has a wonderful texture, with bits of mango floating in it. It's very spicy and terrific

[237]

with stews and curries. *Major Grey's Chutney* is sweet and mild and the *Mango and Ginger Chutney* is a delicious blend of sweet flavors generously spiked with fresh ginger.

The Silver Palate Chutneys—The Silver Palate (a small shop on Columbus Avenue in New York, a best-selling cookbook and a national food company) makes all sorts of delicious condiments, but their chutneys are truly outstanding. The *Apple Mint Chutney* is made from Granny Smiths, onions, fresh mint, lemon juice, raisins, garlic and ginger. Serve it with roast pork, spareribs, ham or lamb. Use it as a stuffing for a boneless breast of chicken or a roast loin of pork. I thought *Blueberry Chutney* sounded like a terrible idea until I tasted this stuff. Fresh blueberries are simmered with a delicious combination of spices to create this very unique condiment. Its sweet, all-American flavor goes well with roast duck, turkey and chicken or as a glaze for ham or pork chops. It's also fantastic on ice cream, waffles, pancakes and cheesecake. Their *Jalapeño Chili Chutney* has got a real bite to it, but it won't overwhelm the flavors in other foods. Slices of hot jalapeño peppers and sweet red and green peppers are mixed with a delicious tomato-onion base. It's excellent on burgers and steaks, sandwiches and barbecued chicken. *Spiced Cranberry Apple Chutney* is a perfect condiment to serve with Thanksgiving or Christmas dinner. The combination of cranberries, apples and crunchy walnuts goes well with turkey, ham, roast duck and chicken. It's also terrific in a turkey or chicken salad.

Wilson's Apple Chutney—"The apple sellers could be heard in the streets of London crying 'Baking apples—two a penny' as early as the 17th century. This apple chutney is a delicious return to tradition—containing freshly picked Bramley's, faithfully cooked to a time-honoured recipe," explains the label on this English chutney. It's thick and chunky with a wonderfully spicy flavor. Serve with roast pork, chicken or ham, or on top of puréed pumpkin or squash.

MAKING YOUR OWN CHUTNEYS

Fresh Coriander-Cashew Chutney

This beautiful pale-green chutney is cooling and refreshing, but also spicy. It's a fantastic combination of Indian flavors—fresh coriander leaves blended with cashew nuts, chile pepper, lemon juice, cumin and yogurt. It takes only minutes to make and is delicious served with grilled chicken, lamb, fish or seafood. It also makes a spicy dip for raw vegetables and fried Indian bread.

1 cup fresh coriander leaves, chopped
1 fresh, small hot green chile pepper, chopped with seeds
3 tablespoons fresh lemon juice
1 tablespoon water
½ cup unsalted cashew nuts, chopped
½ cup plain yogurt
½ teaspoon ground cumin powder
Salt and black pepper to taste

Place the coriander, chile pepper, lemon juice and water into the container of a blender or food processor and blend to form a thick paste. Gradually add the cashews and blend, using a spatula to scrape the mixture down off the sides. Place the paste into a small bowl and mix in the yogurt, cumin and salt and pepper. Place the chutney back into the blender or food processor and blend thoroughly, for about 20 seconds. Place the chutney in a small serving bowl and refrigerate. Serve within 24 hours. *Makes 1 cup.*

Fresh Ginger-Coconut Chutney

The fresh, pungent bite of ginger gives this chutney its distinctive flavor. Serve it with curries, rice dishes, grilled meat, chicken and fish or with Chinese stir-fry dishes. The chutney should be made just before serving; if it's refrigerated, it will only keep about a day.

½ cup peeled and coarsely chopped fresh ginger
¼ cup grated coconut
¼ cup golden raisins
¼ cup fresh lemon juice
1 clove garlic, chopped
1½ tablespoons coconut milk or water
½ teaspoon salt

Place all the ingredients in the container of a blender or food processor and blend about 30 seconds. Using a spatula, scrape the mixture down off the sides of the blender and blend another 45 seconds, or until the mixture forms a thick, chunky puree.

Cover and refrigerate for up to 24 hours. *Makes about ½ cup.*

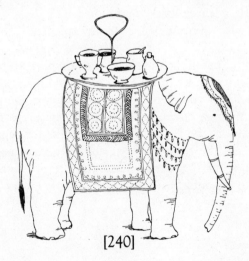

Mango Chutney

This chutney has a wonderful balance of sweet and spicy flavors. Serve it with curries, roast duck, chicken and lamb—or just eat it straight out of the jar. You can easily double or triple this recipe and preserve what you can't eat right away.

1½ to 2 cups thinly sliced underripe mango (about 1 large mango)
2 small green peppers, thinly sliced
½ red onion, thinly sliced
1 large fresh green chile pepper, thinly sliced
½ cup raisins
½ cup freshly squeezed grapefruit juice
1 teaspoon grated grapefruit rind
¼ cup apple cider vinegar
¼ cup brown sugar
¼ cup honey
1½ teaspoons chopped fresh ginger, or ½ teaspoon dried ground ginger
½ teaspoon yellow mustard seeds
½ teaspoon coriander seeds
¼ teaspoon freshly grated nutmeg

Place all the ingredients into a large stainless-steel saucepan and mix well. Let the mixture come to a boil over a high heat. Reduce the heat to low and simmer for about 25 minutes, or until the mixture is thickened and the liquid is syrupy. (If the chutney seems too thin and liquidy, raise the heat to high and let the mixture boil for about 3 or 4 minutes until slightly thickened.) Place the chutney into hot, sterilized mason jars and seal tightly. Process for 20 minutes in a boiling water bath (see pages 216–17 for additional notes on canning), or let cool and place in the refrigerator.

Cranberry, Grapefruit, Ginger and Walnut Chutney

This delicious sweet-and-sour chutney has an incredibly beautiful pinkish-maroon color. The recipe can easily be doubled if you want to make it to give as a Christmas gift.

Serve with roast duck, chicken, turkey or ham, or try it with a turkey or chicken salad or on thin slices of cold ham or roast beef. You could also serve it over vanilla ice cream.

    4 cups whole cranberries (1 pound)
    1 cup grapefruit juice
    1 teaspoon grated grapefruit rind
    ½ cup apple cider
    ½ cup apple cider vinegar
    1 small onion, chopped
    1 tablespoon minced fresh ginger
    1 teaspoon allspice
    1 teaspoon ground cinnamon
 1½ cups maple syrup (or sugar)
    1 cup chopped walnut halves

In a large stainless-steel pot, mix the cranberries, grapefruit juice and rind, apple cider, vinegar, onion, ginger, allspice and cinnamon. Bring the mixture to a boil over a high heat. As soon as it begins to boil, lower the temperature and let the chutney simmer for 10 minutes, uncovered.

Add the maple syrup and, stirring occasionally, let the chutney simmer, uncovered, for 15 minutes or until thickened. Remove from the heat and stir in the walnuts. Let the chutney cool slightly and place in sterilized jars. Cover tightly, let cool, and refrigerate. Use within two weeks. *Makes about 5 cups.*

Karen and Judy's Peach-Mango Chutney

Serve with grilled chicken, lamb curry, on a cheese sandwich or with grilled shrimp.

1½ to 2 pounds slightly soft peaches, peeled and coarsely chopped
1 medium-size, slightly soft mango, peeled and coarsely chopped
1 cup apple cider vinegar
1 cup honey
½ cup fresh orange juice
1 clove garlic, minced
1 tablespoon diced fresh ginger
1 teaspoon cinnamon
1 teaspoon cloves
1 teaspoon salt (optional)

Place all the ingredients in a large stainless-steel saucepan. Bring the mixture to a boil over a high heat, lower the heat and let simmer, uncovered, for 45 minutes, or until thick. (Be sure to stir the mixture every 10 minutes or so to keep it from sticking.) Process for 10 minutes in a boiling water bath (see pages 216–17 for additional notes on canning), or let cool and place in the refrigerator. *Makes about 3 cups.*

Rhubarb Chutney

Thick, sweet-and-sour, this chutney is based on an old English recipe. It's a great way to preserve the flavor of fresh summer rhubarb. Serve with roast pork, duck or goose, or spread on buttered toast with thinly sliced cheddar cheese.

> 2 pounds fresh rhubarb, cut into small 1-inch pieces
> 2 cups white or light brown sugar
> 1½ cups chopped onion
> 1½ cups apple cider vinegar
> ½ cup golden raisins, coarsely chopped
> 1 tablespoon chopped fresh ginger
> ½ to 1 teaspoon salt
> ½ teaspoon cayenne pepper
> ¼ teaspoon ground cinnamon
> ¼ teaspoon ground cloves

Mix all the ingredients in a large, stainless-steel saucepan and place over a moderate heat. Let simmer gently for about 40 minutes, or until the mixture is thickened. Remove the saucepan from the heat and let sit for an hour.

Place the pan over moderate heat and let simmer for an additional 45 minutes. Place the chutney in hot, sterilized jars and seal. Process for 15 minutes in a boiling water bath (see pages 216–17 for additional notes on canning), or let cool and place in the refrigerator. *Makes about 4 cups.*

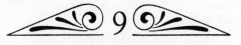

MAIL-ORDER SOURCES

MANY OF THE PRODUCTS discussed in this book are available through the mail. If you have trouble finding these products in your local grocery stores, specialty food shops or ethnic markets, here are the names and addresses of mail-order houses across the country that carry a wide variety of condiments. (Keep in mind that these mail-order houses periodically change their inventories.)

BAILEY'S JELLY KITCHEN
% Mrs. H. A. Bailey
400 South Commerce Street
Natchez, Mississippi 39120
601-445-8452

Write or call to order Mrs. Bailey's hot pepper jellies and sauces.

BALDUCCI'S
424 Avenue of the Americas
New York, New York 10011
212-673-2600

Write for Balducci's catalog, which includes French and Italian olive oils, a wide variety of mustards, French *cornichons*, Fortnum & Mason chutneys and sauces, Subahdar chutneys, Italian balsamic vinegar, sun-dried tomatoes in extra virgin olive oil, and more.

B. F. Trappey's Sons, Inc.
P. O. Box 400
New Iberia, Louisiana 70561-0400
318-365-8281

Send for Trappey's catalog, which includes a variety of hot pepper sauces, pickled tabasco peppers, jalapeño sauce, steak sauce, and Worcestershire sauce.

Callaway Gardens Country Store
Pine Mountain, Georgia 31822
404-663-2281

The Callaway Gardens Country Store catalog includes their own muscadine sauce, red and green pepper jellies, pepper relish, corn relish, watermelon pickle, and more.

Casa Moneo
210 West 14th Street
New York, New York 10011
212-929-1644

Casa Moneo carries a wide selection of Mexican and Latin American condiments, including Mexican hot pepper sauces, vinegars and Goya Spanish olive oil. Write for their catalog.

Casa Peña Blanca Foods
5400 Fleetwood
El Paso, Texas 79932

Write for a copy of Casa Peña Blanca's price list to order their pepper jelly, Texas ketchup, hot chile sauces and chutneys.

CHICO-SAN, INC.
P. O. Box 810
Chico, California 95927
916-891-6271

Chico-San sells a wide variety of Japanese-made condiments including soy sauce, *tamari*, malt vinegar, rice vinegar and sesame oil. Send for their mail-order price list.

CRABTREE & EVELYN, LTD.
P. O. Box 167
Woodstock, Connecticut 06281

Crabtree & Evelyn carries their own brand of English chutneys, Dijon and flavored mustards, flavored and wine vinegars, French olive oils, flavored oils, French walnut oil, herbal jellies and savory sauces. Send $3 for their catalog.

DEAN & DELUCA, INC.
110 Greene Street, Suite 304
Attention: Mail-Order Dept.
New York, New York 10012
800-221-7714

Dean & Deluca sells Guenard hazelnut, almond and walnut oils; balsamic vinegar; French and Italian extra virgin olive oils; Soleillou flavored oils; Romate sherry vinegars; Paul Corcellet's oils, vinegars, mustards and chutneys; Subahdar chutneys; Callaway Gardens relishes; Desert Rose *salsas*; Santa Cruz *salsas*; Harissa Dea; Talko' Texas crisp okra pickles; Honeycup mustard; Innemore Scotch mustard; French *cornichons*; and more. To order, write or call their toll-free number.

Desert Rose Salsa Co.
P. O. Box 5391
Tucson, Arizona 85703
602-743-0450

Desert Rose Salsa makes a medium and hot *salsa*. Write for price list.

Foods of India
Sinha Trading Co., Inc.
120 Lexington Avenue
New York, New York 10016
212-683-4419

Foods of India sells a large selection of Indian chutneys, relishes and pickles.

Hawaiian Plantations
1311 Kalakaua Avenue
Honolulu, Hawaii 96826
800-367-2177

Write or call for Hawaiian Plantations' catalog, which includes their hot pepper jellies, mustards, macadamia nut and pineapple jelly, and sauces.

Katagiri
224 East 59th Street
New York, New York 10022
212-755-3566

Katagiri sells a wide selection of Japanese and Chinese condiments including soy sauce, *tamari*, *teriyaki* sauce, *tonkatsu* sauce, sweet-and-sour sauce, sesame oil, plum sauce, oyster sauce, rice wine vinegars, flavored vinegars, pickled ginger, and more.

LEKVAR BY THE BARREL
H. Roth & Sons
1577 First Avenue
New York, New York 10028
212-734-1110

The H. Roth catalog includes French raspberry, strawberry and wine vinegars; hazelnut and walnut oils; peanut oils; olive oils; Dijon mustards; Subahdar chutneys; Indonesian *sambals;* sate sauce; Chinese fish sauce; soy sauce, sesame oil; Chinese chile oil; oyster sauce; and more.

MACY'S
The Marketplace
151 West 34th Street
New York, New York 10001
212-695-4400

The Marketplace in Macy's carries a large selection of French, Italian and California olive oil and vinegars, a wide variety of mustards (including Chalif's, Pommery and Honeycup), Oriental sauces, hot pepper sauces, chutneys, and Conimex Indonesian chutneys, relishes and *sambals.* To order, call and ask for The Marketplace.

MY GRANDMAMA'S, INC.
Box 1115
Deerfield, Florida 33441
305-421-4312

Write or call to order My Grandmama's pepper or fruit jellies.

NARSAI'S MARKET
385 Colusa Avenue
Kensington, California 94707
415-527-3737

Narsai's sells several varieties of balsamic vinegar, including Balsamico Reggiano Tradizionale, several brands of French and Italian olive oils, mustards, herbal jellies, their own brand of chutneys, sauces, and more. Write or call for mail-order information.

OLD SAN ANTONIO STYLE GOURMET MEXICAN SAUCES
Lazy Susan Foods, Inc.
P. O. Box 10438
San Antonio, Texas 78210
512-534-1330

Call collect for their list of hot pepper sauces and pepper jellies.

STAR MARKET
3349 N. Clark Street
Chicago, Illinois 60657
312-472-0599

Star Market sells a wide variety of Japanese and Chinese condiments including soy sauces, *tamari*, *teriyaki* sauces, *goma* sauce, *tonkatsu* sauce, oyster sauce, *hoisin* sauce, *wasabi*, pickled ginger, and more. Call or write for mail-order information.

THE CHEF'S CATALOG
3915 Commercial Avenue
Northbrook, Illinois 60062
800-331-1750 or 312-480-9400

The Chef's Catalog carries Conner Farms Pickled Vidalia Onions and relish, Honeycup mustard, Pommery mustards and oils, Judyth's Mountain pepper jellies and sauces, La Taste vinegars, balsamic vinegar, Paul Corcellet mustards and vinegars, Old Monk olive oil, Cuisine Perel chutneys and sauces, and more.

THE CHINESE KITCHEN
P. O. Box 218
Stirling, New Jersey 07980

Send $1 for The Chinese Kitchen catalog, which features a wide variety of Oriental condiments including sesame oil, oyster sauce, hot pepper oil, soy sauce, fish sauce, sweet-and-sour sauce, plum sauce, lemon sauce, Chinese vinegars, and more.

THE MEXICAN KITCHEN
P. O. Box 213
Brownsville, Texas 78520
512-544-6028

Write or call the Mexican Kitchen for their catalog, which includes a wide variety of Mexican hot pepper sauces.

THE SILVER PALATE
274 Columbus Avenue
New York, New York 10023
800-847-4747 or 212-799-6340

The Silver Palate catalog features their own chutneys, mustards, oils, vinegars, *cornichons*, pickles, relishes, jellies, preserves, and more.

THE WHIP AND SPOON
161 Commercial Street
Portland, Maine 04101
207-774-4020

The Whip and Spoon carries Guenard almond, hazelnut and walnut oils, Romate sherry vinegar, La Charcutière mustard, Sun

Brand Major Grey Chutney, Sable & Rosenfeld mustards and relishes, Honeycup mustard, Dessaux vinegars, a large selection of French and Italian olive oil, Elsenham sauces, China Bowl Oriental sauces, Balsamic Vinegar of Modena and Pecos Valley *salsas*.

WALNUT ACRES
Penns Creek, Pennsylvania 17862
717-837-0601

Walnut Acres makes their own ketchup, mayonnaise, virgin olive oil, virgin peanut oil, sesame oil, chutneys, pickles, and more. Send for their catalog.

WILLIAMS-SONOMA
Mail Order Department
P. O. Box 7456
San Francisco, California 94120-7456
415-652-9007

The Williams-Sonoma catalog includes Fini balsamic vinegar, Guenard almond, walnut and hazelnut oils, Italian and French extra virgin olive oils (including Emilio Pucci's), Edmond Fallot's Dijon and grainy mustards, Pommery vinegars, Soleillou flavored oils, and more.

ZABAR'S
2245 Broadway
New York, New York 10024
212-787-2000

Write for a copy of the Zabar's catalog, which features a wide selection of imported mustards, olive oils, vinegars, jellies, pickles, Conimex *sambals* and *ketjaps*, hot sauces and other savory sauces.

INDEX

[253]